Close up on Budget Cookery

BETTY HITCHCOCK

Queen Anne Press, London

Illustrations by Hussein Abbo

First published in 1973 by Queen Anne Press Ltd.,
Paulton House, 8 Shepherdess Walk, London N1

Made and printed in Great Britain by
C. Nicholls & Company Ltd.
The Philips Park Press, Manchester M11 4AU

CONTENTS

CLOSE UP ON BUDGET COOKERY

This book has been written to help the housewife with her meal planning and budgeting. Careful buying, cooking and kitchen management all help to save a few pence. This often means extra time shopping around, extra preparation time before cooking and extra time spent using up the bits and pieces in the kitchen. But time spent is money saved, and this book is for the money savers.

The recipes have been costed and divided into sections, so that a meal may be planned according to the money available. As food prices fluctuate, the costings are only approximate, although relevant at the time of writing. It is hoped that this book will be a guide to budgeting and that some of the recipes will be a reminder of the traditional foods we have overlooked during the last few years.

Buying wisely

We are urged to shop around in order to find bargains and thus reduce our food bills. This is not always easy for the elderly or mothers with babies and toddlers. But it is worth keeping an eye open for bargains and special offers and stocking up on these when they occur. Some shops and supermarkets have 'loss leaders'. These are basic food items such as tea, sugar, tinned fruit or similar groceries which are sold at a much reduced price. It is worthwhile taking advantage of these but be strong minded and do not be tempted to buy some of the more expensive items in the same shop.

To buy wisely means planning ahead and not making a haphazard foray into the shops. Try to plan your weekly menus, then make a detailed shopping list of the items required and *keep* to the list. Avoid impulse buying, as this is usually an expensive mistake. If possible, try to keep a little money aside each week to buy a few extras for the store cupboard for emergency meals or entertaining.

Whether to shop at the local corner shop and pay more, or to shop at the nearest supermarket and pay travelling expenses depends upon each individual's circumstances. It is certainly cheaper to make only one or two shopping expeditions each week, rather than buy a few items daily and one is not so easily tempted into haphazard buying. But once at the supermarket it is sometimes cheaper to buy their own branded goods, which are often made by the large manufacturers and are usually something like 2p–3p cheaper.

Bulk buying

This sounds a very attractive way of saving money but before embarking on such a spending spree it is worth considering some of the disadvantages. Most foods deteriorate with storage and, unless suitable space and special conditions are available for perishable foods, they can go bad rapidly. This often means using up the food unnecessarily and extravagantly in order to prevent it being wasted. Canned and packaged groceries keep longer but take up a lot of space. The best way to take advantage of bulk buying is to form a group with several housewives. The food can then be purchased at a cheaper rate and divided as required.

For those with freezing cabinets the problem is not so acute. Many firms sell ready-packed meats, fish, vegetables and fruit for the deep freeze cabinet direct to the consumer. This usually works out cheaper than buying the same product from a retailer, though the cost of running the cabinet should always be considered when calculating the 'saving' involved. An even greater saving can be made by buying a whole or half carcass of meat and cutting and packing it up oneself. Similarly fruit and vegetables grown in the garden or bought in bulk from a local farm or market can be prepared and packaged at home much more cheaply (though reliable instructions should be followed when doing this).

With the store cupboard and freezer packed with cheaply purchased food, there is a tendency to eat far more extravagantly. It is therefore necessary to discipline oneself if full value is to be gained from bulk buying.

Seasonal buying

Most foods can be purchased throughout the year. However, if the foods are imported or specially grown for the out-of-season market, they are usually very expensive and available only at the luxury high street store. Therefore, to keep within one's budget it is sensible to wait until the foods are in season.

The best time for stocking up the deep freeze cabinet with fruits, vegetables, meat and game is obviously when they are at their cheapest and best. Many farms nowadays sell their produce at the farm gate, and it is often worthwhile making a special journey to buy the fresh produce. Similarly, the only time to make preserves economically is when the fruit and vegetables are cheaply available. During the summer months fish can often be purchased straight from the fisherman on the sea shore and, although you may not be able to depend upon the catch, you can depend upon its freshness.

The charts on pages 18–25 show the foods available or in season from month to month. These should be a helpful guide to meal planning and shopping.

Buying meat

Meat is probably the most expensive item of the weekly house-keeping budget. Although it is an important source of protein—an essential ingredient in a healthy diet—other protein foods like eggs, cheese, fish, milk, and nuts are equally beneficial.

Because this book deals with budget cookery, dishes using the prime cuts of meat have been omitted. Recipes include the cheaper cuts of meat, poultry, and offal which, when made into their various dishes, are often more nutritious than those based on the prime cuts.

When buying meat, ask the butcher for guidance, and he will often be able to advise you on which are the best buys and how to use them. The prime cuts are quick to cook and serve, the cheaper cuts usually need more preparation and take longer to cook. Always try to buy small-boned meats, containing a little fat, as lean meat tends to be tough and tasteless.

The following charts give cooking methods or suitable dishes for the cheaper meat cuts. We hope that some of the recipes and suggestions may encourage the cook to make further experiments with these cheaper cuts.

BUDGET CUTS OF BEEF

Joints silverside, brisket, thick flank

Cuts for stewing or braising flank, skirt, chuck, clod, sticking, leg and shin

Minced beef trimmings from joints and bones
N.B. Should not be too fatty or should be freshly minced and used.

Dishes using cheaper cuts

Brisket and Silverside	*Stewing beef*	*Minced beef*
casserole of brisket	steak and kidney pudding	meat loaf
spiced brisket	steak pie	beef roll
rolled braised brisket	beef and vegetable stew	chilli con carné
boiled beef and carrots	curried beef	meat balls
pot roasted silverside	goulash	stuffed vegetables
	carbonnade	minced beef pie
	beef casserole	spaghetti Bolognese

BUDGET CUTS OF LAMB

Joints shoulder, best end of neck, knuckle end of leg, breast

Cuts for stewing or braising best end of neck, middle neck, scrag, half shoulder, breast

Dishes using cheaper cut

Joints	*Stewing lamb*	*Minced lamb*
stuffed breasts of lamb	hot pot	moussaka
crown of lamb	lamb and mint casserole	lamb patties
lamb pie	haricot lamb	risotto
boiled neck with caper sauce	navarin of lamb	
	Irish stew	
	curried lamb	

BUDGET CUTS OF PORK

Joints hand and spring, blade, knuckle, streaky

Cuts for stewing or braising chump chops, spare ribs, streaky, hand and spring

Minced pork pork pieces, knuckle, trimmings from bones

Dishes using cheaper cuts

Joints	*Stewing pork*	*Pork pieces*
stuffed streaky with parsnips	pork and tomato casserole	pork pie galantine
salt pork with peas pudding	devilled pork chops	pâté
pork and sauerkraut	sweet-sour pork	pork loaf
	pork and beans	
	pork with orange and cider	
	cassoulet	

BUDGET CUTS OF BACON

Joints collar, forehock, streaky, slipper

Cuts for stewing or braising forehock, collar, streaky rashers

Minced bacon bacon pieces, streaky rashers, knuckle

Dishes using cheaper cuts

Joints	*Stewing bacon*	*Minced bacon*
forehock in cider	braised collar	bacon burgers
collar with peas pudding	boiled forehock	bacon quiche
	stuffed kebabs	bacon loaf
	bacon casserole	
	bacon and prune hot pot	

SUGGESTIONS FOR OTHER BUDGET MEALS

Poultry and game

Chicken and turkey
chicken envelopes
chicken salad
chicken and rice mould
braised chicken with bacon
chicken paprika
chicken Maryland
devilled chicken
chicken and mushroom
  casserole
casseroled chicken with
  chestnuts
barbecued chicken legs
turkey bonne femme
turkey pie
curried turkey
risotto

Rabbit, hare and pigeon
roast rabbit
rabbit pie
ragout of rabbit
rabbit fricassée
bacon and rabbit casserole
jugged hare
hare pâté
roast hare with bacon
pigeon pie
casseroled pigeons
braised pigeons
pork and pigeon pie
stewed pigeons with steak

Offal

Liver
liver and bacon
stuffed liver
  Française
liver casserole
liver pâté
liver and bacon roll

Tongue
tongue
  Montmorency
braised tongue
stewed lambs'
  tongues
tongue mousse

Head
stewed calves head
pigs head brawn
pork cheese

Tail and tripe
oxtail with
  dumplings
lambkin pie
tripe and onions

Kidneys and hearts
kidney and
  mushroom sauté
gougère
braised kidneys
devilled kidneys
stuffed lambs
  hearts
stewed ox heart
braised lambs hearts

Sausages
toad in the hole
galantine
haselet
pies and rolls
sausage and onion
  casserole

Buying fish

Fish used to be considered a cheap substitute for meat, but this is no longer true. Not only is fish expensive, but most people today have to buy frozen fish, as the fishmonger is fast disappearing from the local high street. All the same, it is good to include fish in menus whenever possible, as it adds variety and extra nutrients to the diet.

The price of fish varies with the time of year and availability. Herrings and mackerel are still very good buys, as they are particularly high in food value. Haddock, plaice and cod can be used for most of the white fish recipes included in this and other recipe books. To make fish into appetising family meals add extra ingredients such as mushrooms, onions, tomatoes and good sauces. Potatoes, stuffings, rice and pasta are also good accompaniments to the dishes and help to make them go further.

Canned fish such as sardines, pilchards, tuna and salmon, though seemingly expensive to buy, can be expanded with extra ingredients to make them into interesting dishes. Canned salmon and tuna make excellent fish pies, pasties, patties and kedgeree. Pilchards and sardines are particularly good for salads, fritters, and fillings for pastry dishes.

Several fish recipes included in this book are suitable for using up left-over fish. With the addition of hard-boiled eggs, cheese, and vegetables good tasty meals can be produced at a much lower cost. It is sometimes worthwhile buying a little extra fish for use in one of these dishes.

Cooking wisely

Apart from careful budgeting and shopping, other aspects of saving money should be taken into consideration. For example there is little difference between the cost of using the various types of cooking stove, but several pence can be saved by using them economically.

When the oven is in use for a certain dish, make sure that the heat is fully utilised. Two or three dishes such as baked puddings, stews, casseroles, fruit, and pies can be cooked together to save both fuel and time. Plan meals so that they are fully cooked in the oven or on top of stove. Make use of a steamer over a large pan, so that two or three vegetables, fish, or a pudding may be cooked together. When making white sauce, make double or treble the quantity required, and keep the remainder in the refrigerator for up to two days. A pressure cooker used for cooking vegetables, fruit, soups, stews and stocks will also help to cut down on the fuel bills.

Another kitchen cooker which serves a useful purpose, especially for a single person or small household, is the lidded electric frying-pan. This can be adjusted thermostatically and used to cook chops, stews, or several items together to make a complete first course.   Although budget cookery means the use of cheaper foods, it has to be remembered that these dishes usually need extra fuel. Stews and casseroles need long cooking; fish, egg and vegetable dishes need extra sauces and garnishes, and home jam making, bottling and deep freezing need extra fuel. So it is important to be aware of this and economise on the fuel wherever possible.

Convenience foods
Ready-packaged, canned and frozen foods are an important part of our everyday shopping. In many cases they are regarded as basic foods and it is difficult to find substitutes. But we pay for the price of convenience, and all this adds to the cost of the foods. So when there is a choice between an elaborately packaged product or a simple functional plastic bag (such as with dried fruits or sugar) choose the simple pack, which usually costs a penny or two less.

Other more complex convenience foods, such as cake mixes and complete meals are poor value compared with their fresh equivalents. Home-made cakes, biscuits and pastries are much cheaper when compared with ready-packaged varieties and are far superior in taste. Packaged and canned meals are useful for emergencies, but are poor value when analysed for their protein content, since they consist mainly of fillers such as rice, pasta or potato. Home-made preserves are cheaper, though this depends on the availability of the fruit and vegetables.

Ready-canned and packaged soups are also expensive when compared with a home-made product. Soups are so easily made, and rarely take longer than half an hour to cook. They are both warming and nutritional and an ideal way of using up chicken carcasses, vegetables and sauces. When the housekeeping money is running low, soup can be made for a few pence and it makes a cheap filling starter to the meal, or with cheese, biscuits and fruit, it makes a good family lunch.

Frozen vegetables are here to stay and are a way of life for many people, especially those who live in towns or flats. With more manufacturers producing frozen vegetables the prices have come down considerably and compare favourably with their fresh equivalent. They are also available all the year round, with very little price fluctuation. They bear no comparison in flavour with their fresh counterparts however, but with the rising cost of labour and transport even fresh vegetables such as cabbage, spring greens and runner beans are climbing into the luxury class.

Kitchen management

Wasted food is an evil and expense which can easily be avoided. If meals are well planned and the left-overs used up in other dishes, very little wastage should occur. Items such as the remains of the Sunday joint or chicken carcass, sauces, gravies and vegetables, can help make another meal. Green vegetables should be discarded. There is little that can be done with them and they have no food value once cooked. Other vegetables, such as onions, potatoes, carrots etc, if sieved or liquidised and well-boiled with gravy or stock, make an adequate family soup, or they can be added to other dishes.

Left-over meats and fish can be used for a variety of dishes and there are many examples of these in this book. As the left-overs should be quickly yet thoroughly reheated, the meats should be finely chopped or minced. It is worth investing in a good mincer for this purpose. When using up left-overs, they should always be used with fresh foods, to make dishes more appetising and nutritious and it also makes them go further too. Freshly cooked vegetables can be added to cottage pies, pastry made for meat pies, and fresh potato used for fish cakes or pies. Bread, cakes and fruit can often be made into interesting puddings or cold sweets, therefore cutting down cost.

All left-overs should be kept in a cool place, perishable foods should be kept in a refrigerator, and they should be used within 24 hours. Left-overs of left-overs should not be reheated and used again, they should be thrown away or given to the birds.

Using the recipes

Throughout the book margarine has been used instead of butter, to keep down the cost of the dishes. Once or twice where butter really improves the flavour of the dish it has been included, though of course in all cases the two fats may be interchanged. Similarly, lard or cooking fats may be used as preferred, and olive oil or vegetable oils can be used.

Stock cubes may be used, where stock has been included in recipes. These will add extra cost to the dish, though many prefer them for their convenience. Home-made stock can be easily made with bones and vegetables. Care must be taken to ensure that it is fresh, it must be boiled rapidly every day. Standard eggs have been used for the recipes, though small or large can be used instead. Grated cheese refers to almost any cheese that can be grated. Cheddar or a mixture gives a good flavour to cheese dishes, and is an ideal way to use up the left-over ends.

Using the book

The recipes have been classified as follows: soups, starters, meat etc. Note that a variety of meals can be made at a reasonable price and are quite suitable for keeping the family well fed. The cheaper dishes have, therefore, been listed first within each section. As a guide for entertaining a party of six, a selection of menus has been included. These show the average cost per person which makes entertaining guests to a supper party at home an enjoyable proposition.

SUPPER PARTY FOR SIX

Average cost per person 15p–20p
(not including salads or vegetables)

Menu 1	£	*Menu 2*	£
leek and potato soup	0·12½	thick lentil soup	0·12
meat loaf	0·65	bacon quiche	0·40
syrup pudding	0·15	apricot cream	0·36
	0·92½		0·98

Menu 3	£	*Menu 4*	£
onion soup	0·14	stuffed tomatoes	0·26
chicken rice mould	0·90	liver and bacon bake	0·68
chocolate sponge	0·16	bread and butter pudding	0·20
	1·20		1·14

DINNER PARTY FOR SIX

Average cost per person 40p–50p
(not including vegetables or coffee)

Menu 1	£	*Menu 2*	£
potted smoked haddock	0·60	onion soup	0·25
crown of lamb	1·25	mussel stew	0·80
raspberry mould	0·60	braised forehock	0·82
	2·45	chocolate Bavaroise	0·60
			2·47

Menu 3	£	*Menu 4*	£
chicken liver pâté	0·50	orange and grapefruit	0·50
crab pancakes	0·80	chicken casserole	1·50
moussaka	1·20	strawberry sponge	0·50
lemon mousse	0·40	caramel custard	0·25
	2·90		2·75

SUNDAY LUNCH FOR FOUR

Average cost per person 35p
(not including vegetables, salads or coffee)

Menu 1	£	*Menu 2*	£
steak and kidney pudding	0·80	boiled collar	1·10
apple snow	0·14	apple pudding	0·15
lemon cream	0·25	blackcurrant sorbet	0·14
	1·19		1·39

Menu 3	£	*Menu 4*	£
curried chicken	0·80	casseroled pigeon	0·85
plum crumble	0·19	apricot cream	0·27
strawberry sponge	0·36	blackberry and apple pie	0·15
	1·35		1·27

Average cost per person 20p–25p

Menu 1	£	*Menu 2*	£
courgette ramekin au gratin	0·33	mushrooms à la Grecque	0·28
flaky chicken envelope	0·70	jugged hare	1·00
apple snow	0·20	blackcurrant sorbet	0·14
	1·23		1·42

Menu 3	£	*Menu 4*	£
minestrone soup	0·26	creamed corn savoury	0·30
chilli con carné	0·90	steak and kidney pudding	0·90
caramel custard	0·22	rice imperial	0·30
	1·38		1·50

Entertaining

All entertaining is expensive, though an informal supper party in the home is one of the nicest forms of entertainment. In spite of the extra cost of the food, it is still much cheaper than going out to a restaurant for a meal. As mentioned earlier, it is a good idea to try to put a few items aside each week in order to have something on which to draw when emergency meals or entertaining looms up. Buy the odd canned luxury when it is on offer and, even better, watch out for the cheap wine offer—which can always be added to the soup, casserole or cold sweet if it is not fit to drink.

Children usually like to have their friends in for tea or the occasional meal. Canned baked beans, beef-burgers and sardines make a good standby for this type of entertainment. Once again, watch out for the bargains and stock up whenever possible. Home-made biscuits and cakes are more filling, nutritious, and half the cost of ready-made ones, so keep the cake tins filled. A large can of ice cream kept in the deep-freeze is a good idea for children's treats and quick puddings.

JANUARY FOODS

Meats

available
turkey
chicken
beef
offal
NZ lamb
NZ lamb's liver
pork
rabbit
pigeon

Fish

best or cheapest	available
crab	bloaters
Dover sole	cod
eel	haddock
mullet	mackerel
sprats	prawns
herrings	skate
plaice	whiting
shrimps	

Vegetables

best or cheapest	available
Jerusalem artichokes	broccoli
chicory	sprouts
watercress	peppers
leeks	cucumber
onions	lettuce
root vegetables	mushrooms
celery	potatoes
	cabbage
	tomatoes

Fruits

best or cheapest	available
pineapple	bananas
tangerines	chestnuts
grapes	grapefruit
forced rhubarb	oranges
cooking apples	lemons
dessert apples	avocado pears
dessert pears	
Seville oranges	

FEBRUARY FOODS

Meats

available
turkey
chicken
rabbit

Fish

best or cheapest	available
crab	bass
Dover sole	bloaters
eel	cod

Vegetables

best or cheapest	available
Jerusalem artichokes	French beans
chicory	cabbage
	peppers

Fruits

best or cheapest	available
imported apples	cooking apples
imported apricots	bananas
	grapefruit

beef
NZ lamb
NZ lamb's liver
pigeon
pork

mullet
plaice
shrimps
salmon
halibut

scampi
haddock
herrings
mackerel
prawns
skate
whiting

watercress
onions
root vegetables

cucumber
lettuce
mushrooms
tomatoes

grapes
pineapple
forced rhubarb

lemons
melon
oranges
avocado pears

MARCH FOODS

Meats

available
beef
English lamb
pork
turkey
chicken
NZ lamb
duckling
pigeon
rabbit
veal

Fish

best or cheapest	*available*
bloaters	hake
cod	kippers
crab	mackerel
sole	mullet
haddock	prawns
herrings	scallops
plaice	
salmon	
shrimps	
whiting	

Vegetables

best or cheapest	*available*
artichokes	sprouts
broccoli	peppers
cabbage	root vegetables
cauliflower	cucumber
chicory	lettuce
cress	mushrooms
onions	spinach
salad onions	potatoes
	tomatoes

Fruits

best or cheapest	*available*
apricots	cooking apples
imported pears	apples
pineapple	bananas
rhubarb	grapefruit
	grapes
	lemons
	oranges
	pears

APRIL FOODS

Meats		Fish		Vegetables		Fruits	
available		*best or cheapest*	*available*	*best or cheapest*	*available*	*best or cheapest*	*available*
beef		bloaters	crab	asparagus	artichokes	imported apples	apples
English lamb		cod	hake	broccoli	aubergine	imported pears	bananas
NZ lamb		sole	kippers	cabbage	old root	rhubarb	grapefruit
pork		haddock	mackerel	cauliflower	vegetables		grapes
turkey		halibut	prawns	cress	peppers		lemons
chicken		herrings	scallops	lettuce	cucumber		melons
duckling		plaice		salad onions	mushrooms		oranges
		salmon		new potatoes	onions		avocado pears
		shrimps			peas		pineapple
		whiting			radishes		strawberries
					spinach		
					tomatoes		

MAY FOODS

Meats		Fish		Vegetables		Fruits	
available		*best or cheapest*	*available*	*best or cheapest*	*available*	*best or cheapest*	*available*
beef		bass	crab	asparagus	broad beans	gooseberries	bananas
English lamb		bloaters	sole	cabbage	French beans	melon	imported apples
NZ lamb		cod	halibut	young carrots	beetroot	rhubarb	cherries
pork		haddock	kippers	cauliflower	courgettes		grapefruit
		herrings					

Continued from previous page:

Meats	Fish	Fish	Vegetables	Vegetables	Fruits
available	*best or cheapest*	*available*	*best or cheapest*	*available*	*available*
chicken	mackerel	mullet	cress	mushrooms	grapes
duckling	plaice	prawns	cucumber	spinach	lemons
pigeon	shrimps	whitebait	lettuce	tomatoes	oranges
rabbit	skate	scallops	peas	onions	avocado pears
turkey	whiting		new potatoes		
			radishes		

JUNE FOODS

Meats	Fish		Vegetables		Fruits	
available	*best or cheapest*	*available*	*best or cheapest*	*available*	*best or cheapest*	*available*
beef	bass	crab	asparagus	cabbage	apricots	apples
English lamb	bloaters	sole	broadbeans	peppers	cherries	bananas
NZ lamb	cod	hake	beetroot	mushrooms	gooseberries	grapefruit
pork	haddock	kippers	carrots	onions	melon	grapes
chicken	herrings	mullet	cauliflower		avocado pears	lemons
duck	mackerel	prawns	cress		imported pears	oranges
goose	plaice	whitebait	cucumber		rhubarb	pineapple
veal	shrimps		lettuce		strawberries	raspberries
turkey	skate		marrow			
rabbit	whiting		peas			
pigeon			new potatoes			
			tomatoes			
			young turnips			

JULY FOODS

Meats	Fish		Vegetables		Fruits	
available	*best or cheapest*	*available*	*best or cheapest*	*available*	*best or cheapest*	*available*
beef	bass	crab	broad beans	runner beans	apricots	imported cooking apples
English lamb	bloaters	sole	French beans	cabbage	blackcurrants	dessert apples
NZ lamb	cod	eel	beetroot	peppers	cherries	gooseberries
pork	haddock	herrings	carrots	mushrooms	melon	grapefruit
chicken	hake	lobster	cress	onions	avocado pears	grapes
duck	halibut	mackerel	cucumber	salad onions	raspberries	greengages
pigeon	kippers	mullet	lettuce	sweetcorn	redcurrants	lemons
rabbit	sole	plaice	marrow		rhubarb	oranges
turkey	sea trout	prawns	peas		strawberries	peaches
veal	shrimps	salmon	new potatoes			imported pears
	whiting	skate	radishes			plums
			spinach			
			tomatoes			

AUGUST FOODS

Meats	Fish		Vegetables		Fruits	
beef	bass	crab	runner beans	cabbage	English dessert apples	English apples
chicken	bloaters	sole	beetroot	carrots	blackberries	bananas
duckling	cod	eel	peppers	cauliflower	blackcurrants	grapefruit
hare	hake	haddock	courgettes	cress		grapes

SEPTEMBER FOODS

Meats

best or cheapest
English lamb, NZ lamb, pigeon, rabbit, pork, turkey

available
beef, chicken, duck, English lamb, NZ lamb, pigeon, pork, rabbit, turkey, veal

Fish

best or cheapest
bass, bloaters, halibut, mullet, salmon, shrimps

available
cod, crab, sole, eel, haddock, herrings, kippers, mackerel, mullet, plaice, skate, whiting

Vegetables

best or cheapest
globe artichokes, aubergines, runner beans, beetroot, peppers, cauliflower, lettuce, marrow, radishes, salad onions, sweetcorn, tomatoes

available
sprouts, cabbage, root vegetables, celery, courgettes, cress, cucumber, leeks, marrow, mushrooms, onions, old potatoes, peas, turnip

Fruits

best or cheapest
English dessert apples, blackberries, damsons, greengages, melon, peaches, avocado pears, English pears, plums, raspberries

available
English cooking apples, bananas, blackcurrants, grapefruit, grapes, lemons, oranges, pineapple, redcurrants, strawberries

OCTOBER FOODS

Meats		Fish		Vegetables		Fruits	
available	*best or cheapest*	*best or cheapest*	*available*	*best or cheapest*	*available*	*best or cheapest*	*available*
beef		bloaters	bass	aubergines	runner beans	dessert and	bananas
chicken		halibut	cod	sprouts	cabbage	cooking apples	blackberries
duck		herrings	crab	cauliflower	peppers	damsons	Brazil nuts
goose		shrimps	sole	celery	root vegetables	chestnuts	grapefruit
hare		sprats	eel	leeks	chicory	peaches	grapes
English lamb			haddock	onions	cress	avocado pears	lemons
NZ lamb			hake	parsnip	cucumber	English pears	oranges
pheasant			kippers		lettuce	plums	pineapple
pigeon			mackerel		mushrooms	walnuts	quince
pork			mullet		salad onions		raspberries
rabbit			mussels		old potatoes		
			plaice		radishes		
			skate		sweetcorn		
			whiting		tomatoes		

NOVEMBER FOODS

Meats		Fish		Vegetables		Fruits	
available		*best or cheapest*	*available*	*best or cheapest*	*available*	*best or cheapest*	*available*
beef		crab	bass	sprouts	globe artichokes	almonds	bananas
chicken		halibut	bloaters	celery	aubergines	apples	grapefruit
duckling		herrings	cod	leeks	beetroot	chestnuts	Brazil nuts

goose
hare
English lamb
NZ lamb
pheasant
pigeon
pork
rabbit
turkey
veal

shrimps
plaice

eel
haddock
hake
kippers
sole
mackerel
plaice
sprats
whiting

onions
parsnip
swede

cabbage
peppers
root vegetables
cauliflower
chicory
cress
cucumber
lettuce
mushrooms
sweetcorn
tomatoes

English pears
plums
strawberries

grapes
lemons
oranges
peaches
avocado pears
pineapple
raspberries
walnuts

DECEMBER FOODS

beef
chicken
goose
hare
English lamb
NZ lamb
pigeon
pork
rabbit
turkey
veal

crab
eel
halibut
herrings
mullet
plaice
shrimps

bass
bloaters
cod
sole
haddock
hake
kippers
mackerel
prawns
sprats
whiting

artichokes
sprouts
celery
leeks
parsnip
swede

beetroot
broccoli
cabbage
peppers
root vegetables
chicory
cress
cucumber
lettuce
mushrooms
old potatoes
tomatoes

almonds
apples
chestnuts
cranberries

bananas
Brazil nuts
grapefruit
grapes
lemons
oranges
peaches
English pears
pineapple
raspberries
walnuts

Minestrone Soup

1 large carrot
1 large onion
1 small swede
1 clove garlic
2 leeks
2 oz margarine
16 oz can tomatoes
1 tsp mixed herbs

$\frac{1}{2}$–1 tsp salt
$\frac{1}{4}$ tsp pepper
2 pt stock
2 tsp tomato purée
small cabbage or
   $\frac{1}{2}$ lb sprouts
2 oz spaghetti
Cheddar cheese

Preparation: 30 min
Cooking: 1$\frac{1}{2}$ hr

Average cost: 26p
Serves: 6–8

Dice carrot, onion and swede into $\frac{1}{4}$ in. pieces, crush garlic and finely slice leeks. Melt fat and fry vegetables about 10 min. Add tomatoes, herbs, spices, stock and purée, leave to simmer about 1 hr. Shred cabbage finely and add to soup with spaghetti broken into 2 in. pieces, continue simmering for a further 30 min. Test for seasoning. Serve with finely-grated cheese.

Leek and Potato Soup

1 medium onion
4 medium leeks
2 oz margarine
1½ pt stock
1 bay leaf

½ tsp salt
¼ tsp pepper
1 medium pkt instant potato
1 tbsp chopped parsley

Preparation: 5 min
Cooking: 25 min

Average cost: 12½p
Serves: 8

Peel and chop onion. Wash and finely slice leeks, wash again thoroughly and shake off surplus water. Melt fat in saucepan, gently fry onion and leeks until nearly soft. Add stock, bay leaf and seasonings. Bring to boil and simmer until tender, about 20 min. Remove from heat, stir in potato powder, return to heat, reboil, adjust seasoning and serve sprinkled with parsley.

Cream of Mushroom Soup

4 oz mushrooms
3 oz margarine
8 oz mushroom stalks
1 large onion
1 pt chicken stock
bouquet garni

¼ tsp salt
pinch pepper
2 oz plain flour
½ pt milk
¼ pt top of milk

Preparation: 20 min
Cooking: 30 min

Average cost: 21p
Serves: 4–6

Wipe mushrooms and slice finely. Cook in 1 oz melted fat until just tender. Remove to use later. Thoroughly wash stalks and finely chop. Peel and chop onion. Sauté in remaining fat for 1–2 min, add stock, herbs and seasonings, bring to boil, simmer 30 min. Strain from pan, remove herbs, sieve or liquidise. Melt remaining fat in pan, stir in flour, cook for 1 min. Gradually add milk stirring thoroughly until sauce thickens. Stir in puréed vegetables, stock, sliced mushrooms and top of milk, reboil and serve with toast.

Spring Consommé

4 carrots
1 small turnip
6 spring onions
2 tbsp shelled peas

2 tbsp shelled beans
16 oz can consommé
2 tbsp sherry

Preparation: 10 min
Cooking: 10 min

Average cost: 22p
Serves: 4–6

Peel and slice carrots, peel and dice turnip into $\frac{1}{4}$ in. pieces, prepare onions and leave whole. Cook all vegetables together for
about 5 min in boiling salted water, strain. Add half can of water
to can of consommé and heat to nearly boiling. Stir in vegetables
and bring to boil. Just before serving stir in sherry.

Onion Soup

3 large onions
2 oz butter
2 pt chicken stock
2 bay leaves
$\frac{1}{2}$ tsp salt

pinch pepper
6 $\frac{1}{4}$ in. slices French bread
2 oz grated Cheddar cheese
1 tbsp sherry (optional)

Preparation: 5 min
Cooking: 20 min

Average cost: 14p
Serves: 6

Peel onions and finely slice into rings. Melt 1 oz butter in saucepan and add onions. Cook onions over low heat until just golden
brown. Add stock, bay leaves and salt and pepper. Simmer gently
about 15 min until onion has cooked. Meanwhile, toast bread
until golden, spread with remaining butter, sprinkle each slice
with grated cheese and brown under grill. Serve at once with
soup. Add sherry to soup just before serving.

Artichoke Soup

1 lb Jerusalem artichokes
1 large onion
1 oz bacon dripping
1 pt stock
½ tsp mixed herbs

¼ tsp salt
pinch pepper
1 oz cornflour
½ pt creamy milk
1 tbsp parsley or chives

Preparation: 20 min
Cooking: 30 min

Average cost: 12p
Serves: 4–6

Peel artichokes and onion and slice. Gently fry in melted fat in covered pan for about 5 min. Add stock, herbs, salt and pepper, bring to boil and simmer about 20 min until tender. Strain and sieve or liquidise vegetables. Return to pan with stock and bring to boil. Blend cornflour with cold milk, stir into boiling liquid and reboil about 2 min. Serve sprinkled with chopped parsley or chives.

Thick Lentil Soup

4 oz lentils
2 medium onions
2 large carrots
1 small turnip
1 large potato
2 stalks celery

1 oz bacon dripping
2 pt stock
bouquet garni
8 oz can tomatoes or
  2 tsp tomato purée
½ tsp salt and pepper

Preparation: 15 min
Cooking: 1½ hr

Average cost: 12p
Serves: 6–8

Wash lentils, prepare and grate vegetables. Melt fat in saucepan, stir in all vegetables and cook for about 5 min, stirring frequently. Add stock, bouquet garni, tomatoes and salt and pepper. Bring to boil and simmer about 1½ hr, thin down with stock or milk and serve with toast or crispy bread.

Anchovy Egg Mayonnaise

4 eggs, hard-boiled
2 tsp anchovy essence
1 lettuce heart
1 pkt cress

4 tbsp mayonnaise or
   thick salad cream
1 tbsp capers or
   8 anchovy fillets

Preparation: 12 min

Average cost: 26p
Serves: 4

Cut the eggs in half lengthways and remove yolks. Mash yolks with essence and 2 tsp mayonnaise and fill back into egg whites. Arrange lettuce and cress on a dish, place eggs cut side down onto dish. Coat eggs with mayonnaise and garnish eggs with capers or anchovy fillets.

Creamed Corn Savoury

4 streaky rashers
2 oz mushrooms
10½ oz can creamed corn

2 eggs
pinch salt
pinch pepper

Preparation: 5 min
Cooking: 5 min

Average cost: 22p
Serves: 4

Dice bacon into ½ in. pieces and fry lightly in pan. Chop mushrooms and add to pan. Fry bacon and mushrooms until just cooked. Stir in creamed corn and heat gently. Whisk eggs and stir into pan adding salt and pepper. Stir until mixture has thickened and cooked. Spoon into 4 individual dishes and serve with toast.

Pepper and Tomato Salad

1 red pepper	French dressing
1 green pepper	*¼ tsp salt*
6 large firm tomatoes	*large pinch pepper*
1 tbsp chopped chives,	*2 tbsp olive oil*
parsley or chervil	*2 tsp vinegar*
	2 tsp lemon juice

Preparation: 10 min   **Average cost: 25p**
                                           Serves: 4

Remove seeds from peppers and slice finely into rings. Dip tomatoes into boiling water for 3 sec, remove skins. Cut tomatoes into slices. Arrange tomatoes and peppers alternately on a dish. To make the dressing mix together salt and pepper and oil. Gradually stir in the vinegar and juice. Spoon over dressing and sprinkle with herbs. Serve chilled with brown bread and butter.

Potted Smoked Haddock

12 oz smoked haddock	*¼ tsp black pepper*
2 oz cooked rice	*2 oz butter*
1 tbsp chopped parsley	

Preparation: 5 min   **Average cost: 35p**
Cooking: 10 min   **Serves: 4**

Poach smoked haddock in water until just cooked. Drain off water and remove skin and bones. Flake fish and break down a little. Mix together fish, rice, parsley and pepper. Melt butter, mix a little with fish mixture and spoon into individual dishes. Pour remaining butter over top and leave to chill. Serve with hot toast.

Chicken Liver Pâté

1 medium onion
1 oz margarine
1 clove garlic
8 oz chicken liver
½ tsp mixed herbs

large pinch salt
large pinch pepper
2 oz butter
1 lemon

Preparation: 5 min
Cooking: 10 min

Average cost: 24p
Serves: 4

Peel and chop onion, lightly fry in margarine until tender. Stir in crushed garlic and cut up liver and herbs, cook gently about 5 min. Remove from heat and mash with a fork until broken down. Place in individual dishes and spoon melted butter over top. Serve chilled with lemon wedges and hot toast.

Savoury Cream Cheese

8 oz Demi sel cheese
2–3 tbsp top of milk
4 spring onions

2 hard-boiled eggs
1–2 tsp curry powder
few potato crisps

Preparation: 10 min

Average cost: 30p
Serves: 4

Mash the cheese in a bowl with milk until soft and smooth. Finely chop onions and stir into mixture with coarsely chopped eggs and curry powder. Spoon into individual pots and sprinkle with crushed potato crisps. Serve chilled.

Courgette Ramekin

1 medium onion
2 oz mushrooms
2 oz cooked bacon or ham
2 oz margarine
1 lb courgettes

¼ tsp salt
pinch pepper
*4 oz finely-grated
    Lancashire cheese*
1 tsp dry mustard
2 tsp Worcestershire sauce

Preparation: 5 min
Cooking: 20 min

Average cost: 22p
Serves: 4

Peel and chop onion, chop mushrooms. Fry together in 1 oz margarine until tender. Stir in chopped ham. Spoon into fire-proof dish. Add rest of margarine to pan and stir in courgettes cut into ¼ in. slices. Add salt and pepper, cover and cook slowly until tender. Remove courgettes from pan, put onto mixture in dish. Drain off liquid in pan leaving about 3 tbsp and stir in other ingredients. Heat gently until runny, then spoon over courgettes. Brown under hot grill.

Mushrooms à la Grecque

1 medium onion
2 tbsp olive oil
2 tbsp cider
2 tbsp white vinegar
bouquet garni
1 clove garlic

½ lb button mushrooms
½ lb small firm tomatoes
¼ tsp salt
large pinch pepper
1 tbsp chopped parsley

Preparation: 6 min
Cooking: 10 min

Average cost: 25p
Serves: 4

Peel and roughly chop onion, fry in 1 tbsp oil until tender. Remove from heat, add cider, vinegar, herbs, crushed garlic and wiped trimmed mushrooms. Return to heat, cover and cook for about 3 min. Peel and quarter tomatoes, add to pan with salt and pepper, cook about 5 min in uncovered pan. Remove from heat, discard herbs and allow to cool. Stir in remaining oil, put into small dishes, sprinkle with parsley and chill before serving with crispbread or toast.

Stuffed Tomatoes

4 large tomatoes
6 rashers streaky bacon
1 small onion
2 tbsp breadcrumbs
2 tsp chopped parsley

pinch salt
pinch pepper
1 oz margarine
4 rounds bread
fat for frying

Preparation: 10 min
Cooking: 30 min

Average cost: 18p
Serves: 4

Cut a slice from top of each tomato and scoop out pulp with a teaspoon. Turn tomatoes upside down to drain. Cut bacon into small pieces and fry gently until just cooked, remove from pan and fry peeled and chopped onion. Mix into the pulp with crumbs, parsley and salt and pepper. Stand tomatoes on baking dish, dot with margarine and cook 30 min at 350°F (mark 4). Meanwhile fry bread until golden and serve tomatoes on fried bread.

Kipper Pâté

½ lb pkt kipper fillets
4 oz butter
½ tsp freshly ground pepper

2 tbsp lemon juice
1 large clove garlic
toast

Preparation: 25 min.

Average cost: 30p
Serves: 4

Remove skin from fish fillets and pound or mince them in a basin. Soften the butter and work in the pounded kipper, pepper, juice and crushed garlic. Put into small dishes and leave to chill. Serve with fingers of hot toast.

Tuna Salad

1 lettuce heart	Garlic dressing
2 oz French beans, cooked	¼ tsp mustard
2 tomatoes	large pinch salt
8 anchovy fillets	pinch pepper
1 can tuna	2 tbsp olive oil
2 hard-boiled eggs	2 tsp vinegar
1 small red pepper	2 tsp lemon juice
8 black olives	1 clove garlic

Preparation: 20 min

Average cost: 50p
Serves: 4

Arrange lettuce and beans on a large dish. Peel and slice tomatoes, halve the anchovies and cut tuna into 1 in. pieces. Put these decoratively onto dish with quartered egg, sliced, deseeded pepper and olives. Make dressing and stir in crushed garlic. Spoon dressing over salad just before serving chilled with brown bread and butter or crispbread.

Orange and Grapefruit Salad

2 grapefruit	½ oz walnuts
2 large oranges	3 tbsp French dressing
1 lettuce heart	½ oz raisins or sultanas
8 oz carton curd cheese	

Preparation: 20 min

Average cost: 36p
Serves: 4

Peel grapefruit and oranges with a small sharp knife to remove all skin and pith. Carefully remove all segments, discard pithy core. Arrange lettuce leaves on individual dishes, put a spoonful of cheese on each dish and arrange grapefruit and orange segments around cheese. Sprinkle with chopped nuts and raisins. Make dressing (see page 31) and pour over each salad.

Stuffed Beef Roll

8 oz piece of beef skirt
2 medium onions
4 oz mushrooms
1 oz dripping
4 oz sausage meat
pinch salt and pepper
½ pt stock

Shortcrust pastry
6 oz plain flour
pinch salt
3 oz cooking fat, lard or
  margarine
1½ tbsp cold water
milk

Preparation: 25 min
Cooking: 1¼ hr

Average cost: 50p
Serves: 4

Flatten beef on board and beat well. Peel and chop onions and mushrooms. Melt fat in large pan and fry mushrooms and onions until just brown. Remove and mix half with sausage meat. Spread onto meat, roll up and tie into shape. Fry gently in remaining fat until well browned, add stock and rest of onion mixture, salt and pepper. Simmer 30 min, remove and cool. Put flour and salt into bowl, rub in fat with fingertips until well mixed, form into firm dough using round bladed knife. Roll into rectangle on floured board 8 in. by 10 in. Wrap round prepared meat. Put into baking dish, brush with milk and bake for 20 min at 400°F (mark 6), cover and bake a further 20 min. Serve with thickened remaining gravy.

Meat Loaf

¾ lb minced lean beef
¾ lb minced cold bacon
6 oz fresh breadcrumbs
¼ tsp salt

large pinch black pepper
pinch grated nutmeg
pinch dry mustard
2 large eggs

Preparation: 20 min
Cooking: 2 hr

Average cost: 65p
Serves: 6–8

Put all ingredients into a bowl and mix well with whisked eggs. Grease 1 lb loaf tin and press mixture into tin. Cover with foil. Stand tin in another deep tin containing water and bake for 2 hr at 325°F (mark 3). Remove from heat and press with weight on top until cold. Turn out and serve sliced with salad. (If preferred loaf may be steamed for 2½ hr.)

Chilli Con Carné

2 medium onions
1 large clove garlic
1 green pepper
2 tbsp vegetable oil
¾ lb raw minced beef
12 oz can tomatoes

1 tbsp tomato purée
1–2 tsp chilli powder
10 oz can red beans
¼ tsp salt
large pinch pepper
4 oz long grain rice

Preparation: 5 min
Cooking: 40 min

Average cost: 65p
Serves: 4

Peel and slice onions, crush garlic. Remove seeds from pepper and finely slice. Heat oil and fry these until tender. Stir in beef and cook until brown, add remaining ingredients except rice and bring to boil. Simmer 30 min, stirring occasionally. Meanwhile cook rice in fast boiling salted water for 12 min, drain and keep hot. Serve chilli con carné with rice and green salad.

Add more or less chilli powder according to taste.

Beef and Vegetable Stew

2 large onions
2 large carrots
1 piece turnip
3 celery sticks
1 lb stewing beef
1 oz dripping

1 oz plain flour
1 pt stock
¼ tsp salt
pinch pepper
1 tsp mixed herbs

Preparation: 25 min
Cooking: 2¼ hr

Average cost: 60p
Serves: 4

Peel and slice onions, carrots, turnips and celery. Cut meat into 1 in. pieces. Melt fat in saucepan and fry meat until brown, remove and fry a few vegetables until brown, remove and put with meat. Fry flour until well browned, stir in stock, salt and pepper and herbs, bring to boil. Return fried meat and vegetables and simmer for 1½ hr. Add remaining vegetables to pan and continue cooking a further 40 min. Serve with potatoes, dumplings or boiled rice.

Steak and Kidney Pudding

1 lb stewing steak	Suet crust
4 oz kidney	8 oz self-raising flour
1 medium onion	½ tsp salt
1 tbsp plain flour	4 oz prepared suet
½ tsp salt	¼ pt cold water
¼ tsp pepper	stock or water

Preparation: 20 min   **Average cost:** 60p
Cooking: 3½–4 hr   **Serves:** 4

Cut meat and kidney into 1 in. pieces and mix with chopped onion, flour, salt and pepper. Make pastry and knead lightly on floured board, cut off quarter for lid. Roll rest of pastry into round large enough to line inside greased 1½ pt basin, press well into place. Put meat filling inside, spoon in 4 tbsp water. Damp pastry edge, roll lid into 6 in. round and fix into place. Cover with foil and steam for 3½–4 hr in a large pan. Re-fill with boiling water as necessary. Before serving cut wedge from pastry and fill pudding with hot stock or water.

Beef Carbonnade with Dumplings

1 lb piece chuck steak	¼ tsp salt and pepper
2 oz dripping	2 tsp mixed herbs
2 large onions (sliced)	4 oz self-raising flour
2 tbsp plain flour	pinch salt
1 clove garlic	2 oz prepared suet
¼ pt water	4 tbsp cold water
¾ pt brown ale	1 tbsp chopped parsley

Preparation: 15 min   **Average cost:** 66p
Cooking: 2 hr   **Serves:** 4

Cut meat into 2 in. pieces and brown in melted fat, remove and fry onion until brown, put with meat. Sprinkle flour into fat and crushed garlic, gradually add water and ale, bring to the boil. Return meat and onion to pan with seasonings and herbs and simmer for 1½ hr. Mix together flour, salt and suet, make into soft dough with water. Form into 8 balls and drop into simmering stew. Cook for 10–15 min. Serve sprinkled with parsley.

Casseroled Brisket

2 lb joint brisket, boned and
   rolled
1 oz dripping
4–6 small onions
4–6 small carrots

$\frac{1}{4}$ tsp salt
pinch pepper
4 peeled tomatoes
$\frac{3}{4}$ pt stock
8 oz can butter beans

Preparation: 15 min
Cooking: 2$\frac{1}{4}$ hr

Average cost: 92p
Serves: 6–8

Wipe meat and brown all over in heated dripping in large fire-proof casserole. Remove meat and fry peeled onions and carrots. Return meat to casserole with salt, pepper, tomatoes and stock, cover and cook for 1$\frac{3}{4}$ hr at 325°F (mark 3). Add butter beans to dish and cook for a further 15 min. Slice meat and serve on vegetables. Left-over meat may be eaten cold or used up following day.

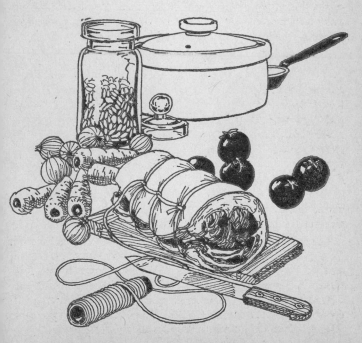

Irish Stew

1½ lb middle and scrag
  neck of lamb
4 medium onions
1 lb peeled potatoes

½ tsp salt
¼ tsp pepper
¾ pt stock or water
1–2 tbsp chopped parsley

Preparation: 10 min
Cooking: 1½ hr

Average cost: 45p
Serves: 4–5

Cut the meat into neat joints between bones. Peel and slice onions and potatoes. Sprinkle with salt and pepper. Arrange layers of meat and vegetables in a casserole or saucepan, finishing with potato layer. Pour over stock, bring to boil and simmer gently for 1½ hr. Remove potatoes from top, arrange meat down centre of dish, with potatoes over top. Mash rest of vegetables in pan and pour over. Garnish with parsley.

Lamb Pie

1 lb lean lamb
2 large onions
¼ tsp salt
large pinch pepper
¼ pt water
1 oz plain flour
¼ pt milk

1 tbsp chopped parsley
8 oz plain flour
½ tsp salt
4 oz cooking fat or margarine
2 tbsp cold water
milk

Preparation: 25 min
Cooking: 1 hr

Average cost: 50p
Serves: 4–6

Cut meat into small cubes, chop peeled onion. Put into pan with salt, pepper and water, simmer gently about 30 min until tender. Blend flour with milk, pour into pan, reboil. Stir in parsley. Make shortcrust pastry (see page 36). Divide in half and roll into 2 rounds. Line 7–8 in. pie plate with one piece, put meat filling inside, damp edges. Fix pastry lid in place, flute and decorate edges. Brush with milk. Bake for 30 min at 400°F (mark 6) until golden brown. Serve hot or cold.

Stuffed Breasts of Lamb

2 small breasts of lamb
2 lambs kidneys
4 rashers bacon
4 tbsp pkt stuffing
2 tbsp milk
1 egg
2 oz dripping

2 onions
6 peeled potatoes
½ tsp salt
¼ tsp pepper
1 tbsp chopped parsley
½ pt stock

Preparation: 25 min
Cooking: 2 hr

Average cost: 60p
Serves: 4

Ask butcher to bone meat, cut off excess fat. Make stock with bones. Peel, core and chop kidneys, fry with chopped bacon until both are tender. Soak stuffing with milk, mix with kidney and blend in egg. Spread stuffing on one breast, place other on top, tie, skewer or sew in place with fine string. Melt fat in baking tin, brown meat on both sides, remove, brown sliced onion and potatoes. Stir in salt, pepper and parsley, put meat on top, pour over stock. Cover with foil, bake for 1½ hr at 350°F (mark 4). Serve with redcurrant jelly.

Lamb and Mint Casserole

2 lb middle neck lamb
8–12 shallots
8–12 young carrots
1–2 young turnips
1 tsp salt
¼ tsp pepper

1 pt lamb stock or water
2 tbsp chopped mint
2 tbsp chopped parsley
8 small new potatoes
4 oz shelled peas
4 oz broad beans

Preparation: 25 min
Cooking: 1½ hr

Average cost: 60p
Serves: 4

Cut meat into neat joints and put into casserole with peeled whole shallots, carrots and quartered turnip. Sprinkle with salt and pepper, add stock, 1 tbsp chopped mint and parsley. Cover and cook for 45 min at 350°F (mark 4). Remove from oven, add potatoes, peas and beans. Cook for a further 45 min. Just before serving add 1 tsp vinegar and sprinkle with mint and parsley.

Navarin of Lamb

8 lamb cutlets
2 medium onions
4 oz mushrooms
1 oz plain flour
1 pt stock

½ tsp salt
¼ tsp pepper
2 peeled carrots
1 peeled small turnip

Preparation: 20 min
Cooking: 1¾ hr

Average cost: 70p
Serves: 4

Trim cutlets and remove excess fat. Melt the fat and fry cutlets until brown on either side. Put into casserole, fry the sliced peeled onions and mushrooms, add to casserole. Sprinkle flour into pan, cook until golden brown, gradually stir in stock, bring to boil. Pour over meat and vegetables, add salt and pepper, cover and cook for 1 hr at 350°F (mark 4). Remove lid, stir in diced vegetables and cook a further 30 min.

Moussaka

1½ lb aubergines
4–6 tbsp vegetable oil
4 medium onions
1 lb lean lamb
4 medium tomatoes
¼ tsp salt

¼ tsp pepper
2 tsp tomato purée
¼ pt lamb stock
2 eggs
4 oz carton single cream

Preparation: 30 min
Cooking: 1¼ hr

Average cost: 75p
Serves: 4

Slice peeled aubergine into ¼ in. pieces. Sprinkle with salt and leave 30 min to draw out liquid. Wipe on kitchen paper. Lightly fry in oil, remove from pan and fry sliced onions. Mince or chop meat and fry for about 3 min. Peel tomatoes and slice. Sprinkle all ingredients with salt and pepper. Arrange in layers in heat-proof dish. Pour over purée and stock, cover and bake for 1 hr at 350°F (mark 4). Whisk together eggs and cream and pour over the mixture. Cook a further 15 min.

Hot Pot

*1 large best end of neck of
  lamb (8 cutlets)*
2 kidneys
2 large onions
4 oz mushrooms

½ tsp salt
¼ tsp pepper
1 lb peeled potatoes
1 tbsp chopped parsley

Preparation: 20 min
Cooking: 1½ hr

Average cost: 75p
Serves: 4

Ask butcher to chine meat and keep bone. Trim off excess fat from joint, then cut into cutlets between the bones. Boil bone with ½ pt water to make stock, strain. Heat fat trimmings in frying pan, remove, fry cutlets until just brown on either side. Halve kidneys, remove core and fry lightly. Pack meat, kidneys, sliced onions, mushrooms, salt and pepper into casserole, pour over stock. Slice potatoes, arrange over top and cover. Cook for 1 hr in oven at 350°F (mark 4), remove lid, dot with fat and cook for further 30 min. Sprinkle with parsley.

Crown Roast

*2 best ends of neck
  (6–7 cutlets each)*
1 medium onion
4 oz mushrooms
1 oz butter
6 oz cooked rice
1 oz raisins

1 oz chopped walnuts
2 tbsp chopped parsley
¼ tsp salt
pinch pepper
2 egg yolks
12 small onions

Preparation: 30 min
Cooking: 1¼ hr

Average cost: £1.25
Serves: 6–7

Ask butcher to make crown with the two joints. Put on a piece of foil in baking tin. Chop onion and mushrooms, cook in butter until tender. Put in bowl with rice, stir in raisins, nuts, parsley and seasonings. Bind together with egg yolks. Stuff into centre of crown, cover with foil and bake for about 1 hr at 375°F (mark 6). Peel and cook onions until tender, drain well. Arrange in centre of crown. Serve with cutlet frills on bones.

Toad in the Hole

1 lb pork sausages (8)   *1 egg*
4 oz plain flour   *¼ pt milk*
pinch salt   *¼ pt water*

Preparation: 10 min   **Average cost: 30p**
Cooking: 45 min   **Serves: 4**

Put the sausages into roasting tin (about 10 in. by 12 in.) Cook in oven for approximately 10 min at 425°F (mark 7) until they have just browned and fat has run out. There should be just about 1 tbsp fat in tin, add extra dripping if necessary or drain away excess fat. Meanwhile put flour and salt in bowl, gradually whisk in egg and milk. Beat thoroughly until smooth, then add water. Pour over hot sausages and return to oven to bake for 35 min until well risen, crisp and brown. Serve with green vegetable.

Devilled Pork Chops

4 pork chump chops   *2 tbsp Worcestershire sauce*
4 oz long grain rice   *2 tbsp chutney*
  pinch salt
Devil paste   *2 tsp curry powder*
1–2 oz pork dripping   *pinch cayenne pepper*
1 tsp tomato purée

Preparation: 10 min   **Average cost: 70p**
Cooking: 20 min   **Serves: 4**

Cut excess fat from chops, melt and put aside dripping to use for devil paste. Gently grill chops so that they are cooked through to centre, but not overbrowned on outside. (Make grill really hot, then turn low when cooking meat.) Meanwhile boil rice in fast boiling salted water for 12 min. Mix together ingredients for devil paste and spread over the 4 chops. Finish cooking chops under hot grill. Serve with rice and green salad.

Sweet-Sour Pork

1½ lb belly of pork	2 tbsp vinegar
1 clove garlic	pinch salt and pepper
1 medium onion	1 oz brown sugar
1½ oz plain flour	2 tbsp lemon juice
1 pt pork stock	1 oz raisins
2 tsp mustard	

Preparation: 10 min   **Average cost:** 65p
Cooking: 45 min   **Serves:** 4

Remove bones from joint and cut meat into 8 slices. Fry on both sides until just brown. Overlap slices into a shallow fireproof dish. Fry crushed garlic with peeled and chopped onion until tender. Stir in flour and brown. Gradually add stock (made from bones), bring to the boil and stir until thickened, remove from heat. Mix together other ingredients and stir into sauce. Pour over pork slices, cover with foil and cook for 40 min at 350°F (mark 4). Serve with creamed potatoes and green vegetable.

Pork and Tomato Casserole

4 spare rib cutlets	¼ tsp salt
1 medium green pepper	pinch pepper
4 medium tomatoes	½ oz butter
1 large clove garlic	2 oz fresh crumbs
1 tsp dried marjoram	4 oz long grain rice

Preparation: 10 min   **Average cost:** 72p
Cooking: 40 min   **Serves:** 4

Remove excess fat from pork, put into pan to melt. Remove brown pieces and fry cutlets until brown on both sides. Put into shallow casserole to hold them in one layer. Remove seeds from pepper. Peel and chop tomatoes, mix with crushed garlic, chopped pepper, marjoram, salt and pepper. Spread over cutlets, cover and bake for 30 min at 350°F (mark 4). Meanwhile melt butter in pan, fry breadcrumbs until golden. Remove casserole lid, sprinkle in crumbs and cook a further 5 min before serving with boiled rice.

Stuffed Pork with Parsnips

2 lb joint belly of pork
2 tbsp sage and onion
    stuffing
1 egg yolk

1 lb parsnips
1–2 oz dripping
1 tbsp chopped parsley

Preparation: 10 min
Cooking: 1¼ hr

Average cost: 70p
Serves: 6

Ask butcher to score skin of pork and to remove bones. Use bones to make stock for gravy. Make stuffing as directed on packet adding egg yolk to bind it together. Make a slit through the streaky layers of meat and push in stuffing. Tie or stitch with string to hold together. Put into baking tin and roast for 30 min at 400°F (mark 6) then reduce heat to 350°F (mark 4) for a further 45 min. Meanwhile peel and cut parsnips into even-sized pieces, boil 5 min in salted water. Drain and roast in tin with pork, turn frequently. Serve sprinkled with parsley.

Bacon Quiche

*4 oz streaky bacon or
  bacon pieces*
1 medium onion
6 oz shortcrust pastry

2 eggs
¼ pt milk
pinch salt and pepper
4 oz Cheddar cheese

Preparation: 15 min
Cooking: 35 min

Average cost: 25p
Serves: 4

Derind bacon and cut into small pieces, gently fry until just cooked. Remove from pan and lightly fry peeled and chopped onion, remove and put with bacon. Make shortcrust pastry (see page 36) and roll out and line 7 in. flan ring or sandwich tin. Put bacon and onion in base. Whisk together eggs and milk. Stir in salt, pepper and finely grated cheese. Pour into flan ring and bake for 20 min at 400°F (mark 6). Reduce heat to 325°F (mark 3) and cook a further 10–15 min until brown and just set.

Bacon Burgers

*8 oz thinly sliced streaky
  bacon*

12 oz sausage meat
2 medium onions

Preparation: 10 min
Cooking: 35 min

Average cost: 35p
Serves: 4

Remove rinds and gristle from bacon, reserve 8 rashers and finely chop remainder. Fry rinds to remove fat, then lightly fry chopped bacon and put with sausage meat. Fry peeled and chopped onion until tender and just brown. Mix together bacon, sausage meat and onion and form into 8 flat cakes. Wrap bacon rashers around the sides of each cake and secure with cocktail stick. Bake for 20–25 min at 350°F (mark 4) until brown. Serve with tomato sauce.

Stuffed Bacon Kebabs

4 thin sausages
8 thinly sliced bacon rashers
6 oz mushrooms
4 small tomatoes

1 oz bacon fat
4 oz long grain rice
2 tbsp chopped parsley

Preparation: 10 min
Cooking: 12 min

Average cost: 32p
Serves: 4

Grill or fry the sausages until just cooked (left-over sausages may
be used), cut in half and wrap in bacon rashers. Thread on to
4 skewers alternately with 8 small mushrooms and tomatoes, brush
with melted bacon fat. Meanwhile cook rice in fast boiling
salted water for 12 min. Chop remaining mushrooms and fry in
fat, mix with rice and parsley. Grill kebabs until all ingredients
are brown and cooked. Serve on the prepared rice.

Braised Forehock in Cider

2½ lb forehock joint boned and
   rolled
2 bay leaves
2 medium onions

2 carrots
1 leek
½ pt cider
pinch pepper

Preparation: 10 min
Cooking: 1½ hr

Average cost: 82p
Serves: 8

Soak bacon in cold water for 12 hr. Put into pan, cover with
water, add bay leaf, bring to boil and simmer for ¾ hr. Peel and
chop vegetables and fry in fat until brown. Put into casserole.
Remove bacon and strip off rind, put onto vegetables, pour on
cider, add pepper and bay leaf. Cover and bake for 30 min at
350°F (mark 4). Remove lid and cook a further 15 min to brown.
Left-over bacon may be served cold or used for one of 'left-over'
dishes.

Lamb Tongues Montmorency

6 lamb tongues
2 oz dripping
1 large onion
1 large carrot
2 celery stalks

2 oz plain flour
¾ pt stock
12 oz can black cherries
pinch salt and pepper
1 tbsp redcurrant jelly

Preparation: 15 min
Cooking: 1¼ hr

Average cost: 50p
Serves: 4

Boil tongues in water for 20 min. Remove and take off skin. Meanwhile melt fat, fry prepared and diced vegetables until brown, put into casserole, place halved tongues on top. Add flour to pan, brown, gradually add stock and 4 tbsp juice from drained cherries, bring to boil, add salt, pepper and redcurrant jelly. Pour into casserole. Cook for 45 min at 350°F (mark 4). Add cherries and cook a further 10 min before serving with boiled potatoes.

Kidney and Mushroom Sauté

4 rashers bacon
4 oz button mushrooms
1 medium onion
8 lambs kidneys
¼ tsp salt

pinch pepper
1 oz plain flour
½ pt stock
1 tsp tomato purée

Preparation: 10 min
Cooking: 20 min

Average cost: 45p
Serves: 4

Chop bacon and fry lightly, remove and fry mushrooms (whole) and peeled and chopped onion until just tender. Remove and put with bacon. Toss peeled, halved and cored kidneys in seasoned flour, fry in remaining fat until brown and cooked (about 7 min). Add remaining flour and brown. Gradually stir in stock and purée, bring to boil and simmer. Return all ingredients to pan, reheat for 10 min. Serve in hot dish surrounded by croutons of fried bread.

Liver and Bacon Bake

12 oz lambs liver (8 slices)
2 oz fresh breadcrumbs
1 tbsp chopped parsley
large pinch salt
small pinch pepper

½ tsp mixed herbs
1 egg
8 oz bacon rashers
½ pt stock

Preparation: 15 min
Cooking: 40 min

Average cost: 46p
Serves: 4

Put slices of liver in shallow fireproof dish. Mix together crumbs, parsley, salt, pepper, herbs and egg to make stuffing. Spread a little stuffing on each liver slice. Cover each with bacon rasher, pour stock round dish, cover with foil. Bake for 30 min at 350°F (mark 4). Remove foil and cook a further 10 min to brown bacon.

Stuffed Braised Hearts

4 small lambs hearts
4–6 tbsp thyme and parsley stuffing
2 oz dripping
1 large onion
2 celery stalks
1 large carrot

1 small turnip
2 oz plain flour
¼ tsp salt
pinch pepper
¾ pt stock
1 tsp tomato purée

Preparation: 20 min
Cooking: 1½ hr

Average cost: 40p
Serves: 4

Wash hearts, dry well and cut through central division to form cavity. Make stuffing and fill into each heart. Tie or stitch together with fine string. Melt fat, dip hearts in flour and fry until browned all over. Remove, fry prepared and sliced vegetables until brown. Remove, fry seasoned flour until brown, stir in stock and purée, boil until thickened. Put vegetables back into pan with hearts on top, cover and simmer for 1–1¼ hr.

Stewed Oxtail with Savoury Dumplings

1 oxtail	*1 stick celery*
2 oz plain flour	*2 tsp mixed herbs*
½ tsp salt	*1½ pt stock*
¼ tsp pepper	*4 oz self-raising flour*
2 oz dripping	*pinch salt*
1 large onion	*1½ oz prepared suet*
1 large carrot	*4 tbsp cold water*

Preparation: 15 min　　**Average cost: 82p**
Cooking: 2½ hr　　**Serves: 4–5**

Cut oxtail into joints, dip into seasoned flour and brown in melted fat. Prepare and slice vegetables. Remove meat and fry vegetables until brown. Remove vegetables from pan. Fry remaining seasoned flour until brown and stir in stock and 1 tsp herbs. Return meat and vegetables to pan, bring to boil and simmer for 2–2½ hr. Mix together remaining ingredients and form into dough with water, divide into 8 and drop on top of stew, cook for a further 10–15 min.

Shepherd's Pie

1 lb potatoes or
   3 oz pkt instant potatoes
1 large onion
1 oz dripping
1 oz plain flour

½ pt stock
2 tsp tomato purée
8 oz cold lamb
2 oz cooked bacon
salt and pepper

Preparation: 30 min
Cooking: 35 min

Average cost: 30p
Serves: 4

Peel and cook potatoes and cream, or make up mashed potato. Peel and chop onion, fry in melted fat. Stir in flour and cook until brown. Stir in stock and purée and bring to boil. Finely chop or mince lamb and bacon, mix into gravy and season to taste. Put into pie dish. Beat pinch nutmeg into potatoes and spread over meat. Dot with some flaked fat and bake for 30 min at 375°F (mark 5) until brown.

Savoury Pancakes

4 oz plain flour
¼ tsp salt
1 egg
½ pt milk
¼ pt water
1–2 oz lard or vegetable fat

1 oz margarine
1 oz plain flour
pinch pepper
12 oz can tomatoes
8 oz left-over cooked bacon
1 oz grated cheese

Preparation: 25 min
Cooking: 10 min

Average cost: 30p
Serves: 4

Mix flour and salt. Whisk together egg and half milk, gradually stir into flour to form a batter, beat well, then add water. Fry 8 small pancakes in fat. Keep hot. Melt margarine, stir in flour, add remaining milk, pepper and ¼ pt juice drained from tomatoes. Bring to boil, stirring until thickened. Stir in the minced or chopped bacon. Put 1–2 tbsp of mixture onto each pancake, roll up and put into hot dish. Pour over tomatoes, sprinkle with cheese and brown under grill.

Savoury Plate Pie

8 oz shortcrust pastry	2 tsp tomato purée
1 medium onion	2 tsp Worcestershire sauce
1 oz dripping	8 oz cooked meat
1 oz plain flour	salt and pepper
½ pt stock	milk to glaze

Preparation: 20 min   Average cost: 35p
Cooking: 40 min   Serves: 4

Make pastry (see page 36), divide in half and roll each portion into 8 in. round. Line 7 in. pie plate with one half, damp edges. Peel and slice onion into rings and fry in fat until tender, drain off fat and place in prepared pastry. Add flour to pan and fry until brown, stir in stock, purée and sauce, bring to the boil. Stir into minced meat, adding salt and pepper to taste. Spread over onion rings. Cover with pastry lid, glaze with milk and bake for 30 min at 400°F (mark 6).

Stuffed Marrow

1 medium onion	pinch salt
1 oz dripping	pinch pepper
2 oz mushrooms	8 oz cooked meat
1 oz plain flour	1 medium marrow
¼ pt stock	

Preparation: 20 min   Average cost: 35p
Cooking: 1–1½ hr   Serves: 4

Peel and chop onion and fry until tender in melted fat. Remove and fry chopped mushrooms. Stir in flour and cook until brown, gradually add stock, salt and pepper and cooked minced meat. Meanwhile peel marrow whole, cut off one end and scoop out seeds. Re-fill cavity with meat filling, put into baking dish, pour water round marrow, sprinkle with salt. Cover with foil and bake at 350°F (mark 4) for 1–1½ hr according to size and age of marrow.

Meat Pasties

8 oz shortcrust pastry
8 oz cooked meat
2 medium onions
1 medium potato

1 tbsp chopped parsley
2 tbsp left-over gravy
salt and pepper
milk to glaze

Preparation: 30 min
Cooking: 30 min

Average cost: 35p
Serves: 4

Make pastry (see page 36) divide into 4 and roll each into a round about 6 in. in diameter, damp edges. Dice or mince meat. Peel and dice onions and potato, cook together in a little salted water until tender. Drain and mix with meat, parsley and gravy, adding salt and pepper if necessary. Put a spoonful of mixture in centre of each pastry round, fold one side over to opposite side, press edges well together. Put onto baking tray, brush with milk. Bake for 20 min at 400°F (mark 6) until well browned. Serve hot or cold.

Bean and Sausage Casserole

2 medium onions
1 clove garlic
4 oz streaky bacon
20 oz can baked beans
12 oz cooked sausages

8 oz can corn
4 tbsp cider
1 oz browned crumbs
1 oz grated Cheddar cheese

Preparation: 10 min
Cooking: 25 min

Average cost: 40p
Serves: 4-6

Peel and slice onion and crush garlic. Fry with the chopped bacon until tender in a large frying pan with a lid. Stir in beans, cut up sausages, corn and cider, bring to simmering and cover with lid. Cook for 20 min. Sprinkle with crumbs and cheese, put under grill to brown.

Meat Fritters

12 oz can chopped ham and
   pork loaf, luncheon meat
   or tongue
4 oz plain flour
pinch salt
1 egg

$\frac{1}{4}$ pt milk and water
frying oil
1 medium onion
1 oz butter
12 oz can tomatoes
1 tsp mixed herbs

Preparation: 10 min
Cooking: 10 min

Average cost: 40p
Serves: 4

Cut meat into 8 slices. Put flour and salt together in bowl, whisk in egg and milk and water, beat well to form coating batter. Heat oil in frying pan (it should be about $1\frac{1}{2}$ in. in depth). Meanwhile peel and chop onion, cook in butter in saucepan until soft, add tomatoes, herbs, salt, pepper and sugar. Simmer 10 min and sieve or mash for sauce. Dip meat slices in batter and fry in hot oil until brown and crisp. Drain well and serve with sauce.

Curried Lamb

1 large onion
1 cooking apple
1 oz dripping
1 tbsp curry powder
1 oz plain flour
$\frac{1}{4}$ pt stock

$\frac{1}{4}$ tsp salt
2 tsp tomato purée
1 tbsp chutney
1 oz sultanas
8–12 cold slices lamb
4–6 oz long grain rice

Preparation: 10 min
Cooking: 35 min

Average cost: 50p
Serves: 4–6

Peel and chop onion and apple. Fry until tender in melted fat. Add curry powder and cook 2–3 min. Stir in flour and cook until brown. Gradually stir in stock, salt and purée, bring to boil stirring until thick. Add chutney and sultanas and slices of meat. Simmer gently 30 min. Meanwhile cook rice in fast boiling salted water for 12 min. Serve with extra chutney and sliced banana.

Flaky Chicken Envelope

½ chicken (1½–1¾ lb)
1 small onion
1 bay leaf
large pinch salt
pinch pepper
½ pt water

1 oz margarine
1 oz plain flour
2 tsp chopped parsley
2 oz chopped ham or bacon
12 oz puff pastry
1 egg for glazing

Preparation: 40 min
Cooking: 20 min

Average cost: 70p
Serves: 5–6

Cook chicken with vegetables and water about 40 min. Remove flesh from bones and cut into 1 in. pieces, strain stock. Melt fat, stir in flour, gradually stir in just under ½ pt stock, boil, season and stir in chicken, parsley and ham. Cool. Roll pastry to 12 in. square, trim. Put filling in centre, overlap corners over filling to form envelope, brush edges and top with whisked egg. Put on baking tray. Bake for 10 min at 425°F (mark 7), cover with foil and cook another 10 min. Serve hot with green salad.

Chicken Mayonnaise Salad

½ chicken (1½–1¾ lb)
2 oz butter
4 oz mushrooms
½ lb cooked small new
   potatoes

¼ pt mayonnaise
2 tsp horseradish cream
2 eggs
2 cos lettuce hearts

Preparation: 20 min
Cooking: 45 min

Average cost: 60p
Serves: 4

Rub chicken with butter and roast for 45 min at 375°F (mark 5), leave to cool. Remove flesh from bones and cut into 1–1½ in. pieces. Slice mushrooms and fry in butter until tender, put with chicken. Slice potatoes, hard boil eggs and add horseradish to mayonnaise. Toss meat, mushroom and potatoes in half mayonnaise. Arrange lettuce on dish with chicken mixture on top. Coat with remaining mayonnaise and decorate with sieved egg.

Chicken and Rice Mould

1½ lb chicken pieces
2 onions
½ tsp salt
large pinch pepper
1 oz unsalted butter
1 tbsp oil

4 oz mushrooms
6 oz long grain rice
1 tbsp tomato purée
2 eggs
4 oz Cheddar cheese

Preparation: 30 min
Cooking: 1 hr

Average cost: 60p
Serves: 4

Cook chicken with 1 onion, salt and pepper and 1½ pt water until tender. Drain off stock, dice chicken flesh. Heat butter and oil in frying pan and fry other chopped onion and mushrooms. Stir in rice and fry until well browned. Add 1¼ pt stock, purée and seasoning, bring to boil and simmer until rice cooked and liquid absorbed. Remove from heat, stir in chicken and whisked eggs. Press into ring mould and steam 30 min. Turn onto hot dish. Serve with grated cheese.

Devilled Chicken Legs

4 large chicken drumsticks
1 carrot
1 onion
½ pt stock
pinch salt and pepper
4 oz margarine
3 tsp curry powder

2 tbsp chutney
1 tbsp Worcestershire sauce
1 tsp tomato purée
potato crisps
watercress
chicory

Preparation: 10 min
Cooking: 25 min

Average cost: 60p
Serves: 4

Simmer chicken legs with onion, carrot, stock and seasoning until tender (about 30 min). Remove chicken and cool. Soften margarine and beat in curry powder, chutney, Worcestershire sauce and purée. Make a few slits in leg joints, and spread devil paste over legs and in slits. Heat grill and cook chicken legs until well browned. Serve with potato crisps, watercress and chicory salad.

Fried Chicken

4 chicken pieces
1 oz plain flour
¼ tsp salt
pinch pepper
6–8 tbsp frying oil
4 oz button mushrooms

1 oz butter
1 medium onion
8 oz can tomatoes
1 tsp mixed herbs
1 tsp tomato purée
pinch salt and pepper

Preparation: 10 min
Cooking: 15 min

Average cost: 75p
Serves: 4

Wipe joints and toss in flour, salt and pepper. Heat oil and gently fry chicken until golden and cooked through (about 10–15 min). Wipe mushrooms and fry in small pan until brown and cooked, remove and keep hot. Fry peeled and chopped onion in remaining fat, stir in tomatoes, herbs, purée, salt and pepper. Simmer for 10 min. Drain chicken on kitchen paper before serving with mushrooms and tomato sauce.

Curried Chicken

3–3½ lb chicken
2 oz unsalted butter
1 large onion
1 large garlic clove
2 tsp curry powder

1 oz plain flour
pinch salt and pepper
1 tbsp chutney
2 tsp tomato purée
4 oz long grain rice

Preparation: 20 min
Cooking: 1¼ hr

Average cost: 80p
Serves: 4–6

Cut chicken into 4–6 portions, put skin, bones and giblets in pan with water to make stock. Melt butter and gently fry peeled and sliced onion and crushed garlic. Remove and fry curry powder for 2–3 min, add chicken pieces, remove from pan. Stir in flour, cook for 2 min, gradually stir in stock until sauce has thickened. Add salt, pepper, chutney and purée. Return chicken and onion to pan, simmer for about 1 hr until tender. Serve with boiled rice and extra chutney.

58

Braised Chicken with Bacon

2½–3 lb chicken
2 tbsp oil
2 medium onions
2 medium carrots
1 small turnip
2 celery stalks
2 oz mushrooms

1 tsp mixed herbs
4 oz streaky rashers
1 oz plain flour
¾ pt chicken stock
¼ tsp salt
pinch pepper

Preparation: 20 min
Cooking: 1¼ hr

Average cost: 80p
Serves: 4

Wipe chicken. Simmer giblets in water for stock. Heat oil in fireproof casserole or pan and fry chicken until well browned. Peel and dice vegetables, mix with herbs. Remove rind and halve bacon, fry until brown, put with chicken. Brown vegetables in pan, stir in flour and brown. Gradually stir in ¾ pt chicken stock, add salt and pepper. Return chicken and bacon to pan, cover and cook for 1¼ hr at 350°F (mark 4). Serve with rice or noodles.

Chicken Paprika

2½–3 lb chicken
¼ tsp salt
pinch pepper
2 medium onions
1 large clove garlic
4 medium tomatoes

1 green pepper
1 oz butter
2 tbsp oil
1 tbsp paprika pepper
1 oz cornflour
1 carton yoghurt

Preparation: 20 min
Cooking: 1 hr

Average cost: 90p
Serves: 4

Cut chicken into 4 and put skin, trimmings and giblets to cook for stock. Season chicken, peel and slice onions, remove seeds from pepper, crush garlic and slice peeled tomatoes and pepper. Heat butter and oil in large frying pan. Fry onion and garlic until tender, stir in paprika and fry for about 1 min, stir in ½ pt chicken stock. Put chicken and other vegetables in pan and cover with lid, simmer about ¾ hr until tender. Thicken sauce with cornflour blended with 2 tbsp water, reboil, stir in yoghurt and serve with rice or potatoes.

Chicken Maryland

4 chicken pieces
2 eggs
4 oz fresh breadcrumbs
2 small bananas
frying oil

3 oz self-raising flour
pinch salt
1 egg
8 oz can sweet corn
watercress

Preparation: 30 min
Cooking: 13 min

Average cost: 90p
Serves: 4

Wipe joints, dip into whisked eggs and toss in breadcrumbs, pat crumbs into joints, put into frying basket. Peel and halve bananas, then coat with egg and crumbs. Put flour and salt into bowl, add corn and whisked egg. Mix to a stiff batter with water if necessary. Heat large deep pan of frying oil to 365°F (a cube of bread will turn golden brown in 45 sec). Fry chicken for 8–10 min, bananas for 2 min. Remove and drain on kitchen paper. Reheat oil, drop spoonfuls of fritter mixture into it and cook 3 min until golden and crisp. Drain and serve with watercress salad.

Casseroled Chicken with Chestnuts

3½–4 lb chicken
4 streaky bacon rashers
1 tbsp oil
2 medium onions
¼ tsp salt

large pinch pepper
2 bay leaves
¾ pt stock
½ lb chestnuts
1 tbsp chopped parsley

Preparation: 15 min
Cooking: 1½ hr

Average cost: £1.00
Serves: 4–5

Boil chicken giblets for stock, truss chicken. Lightly fry diced bacon until just cooked, remove from pan, add oil and fry whole chicken until brown. Remove and fry peeled and sliced onions until brown. Drain off fat, return chicken and bacon to pan, sprinkle with salt, pepper and bay leaves. Pour over ¾ pt stock, cover and simmer 30 min. Meanwhile snip chestnuts and boil in water for 5 min, remove from heat and skin. Put chestnuts with chicken and cook for a further 45 min. Serve sprinkled with parsley.

Turkey Pie

2 cooked turkey thighs
2 large onions
½ tsp salt
pinch pepper

½ oz cornflour
2 tbsp milk
2 tsp dried sage
6 oz shortcrust pastry

Preparation: 35 min
Cooking: 50 min

Average cost: 65p
Serves: 4–5

Remove meat from bones and cut into 1 in. pieces. Put bones into pan with peeled and sliced onions, salt and pepper. Add ½ pt water, bring to boil, simmer until onions have cooked. Remove bones. Blend cornflour with cold milk, stir into onions, reboil, stirring until thickened. Remove from heat, add turkey and sage. Pour into 8 in. pie plate or shallow dish. Make pastry (see page 36), roll into 9 in. round, put pastry strip round the edge of plate, dampen, then put on pastry lid. Brush with milk. Bake for 20 min at 400°F (mark 6), cover with foil and cook a further 20 min.

Turkey Casserole Bonne Femme

2 oz bacon dripping
4 turkey portions
3 oz slice streaky bacon
12 small onions
4 oz button mushrooms

1 oz plain flour
¾ pt stock or water
¼ tsp salt
pinch pepper
parsley or watercress

Preparation: 25 min
Cooking: 1¼ hr

Average cost: 80p
Serves: 4

Melt fat in fireproof casserole and fry turkey portions until brown. Meanwhile remove rind from bacon and cut into ½ in. strips, peel onions and leave whole. Boil onions and bacon together for 5 min, drain. Remove turkey and fry bacon, onions and mushrooms in casserole until brown. Sprinkle in flour, cook until brown then stir in stock or water, salt and pepper. Put turkey back into casserole and cook for 30 min at 350°F (mark 4). Drain potatoes and add to casserole, cook a further 30 min. Serve sprinkled with chopped parsley or watercress.

Roast Hare with Bacon

1 young hare
4 tbsp packet stuffing
(parsley and thyme or
sage and onion)

bacon dripping
8 rashers streaky bacon

Preparation: 25 min
Cooking: 1½ hr

Average cost: 75p
Serves: 4–6

Wash inside of cleaned hare and dry thoroughly. Make stuffing and fill cavity, stitch or skewer together. Rub hare with bacon fat or dripping, and skewer into good shape. Put into roasting tin, cover with foil, cook for 1–1½ hr at 350°F (mark 4), basting frequently. Remove rind from bacon and make into 16 bacon rolls, thread onto skewer. About 10 min before serving, remove foil from hare, put rolls to cook and brown. Serve garnished with bacon rolls and gravy made from juices in tin.

Jugged Hare

1 medium hare
3 oz plain flour
1 tsp salt
¼ tsp pepper
4 oz streaky bacon
3 onions

bouquet garni
2 tsp grated lemon rind
4 tbsp port or red wine
6 tbsp lemon and thyme
   stuffing
fat for frying

Preparation: 35 min
Cooking: 2½ hr

Average cost: £1.00
Serves: 6–8

Cut hare into joints and toss in flour, salt and pepper. Brown in melted fat with diced bacon. Put into large casserole with onions, herbs, liver and lemon rind, cover with water, put on lid and simmer for 2 hr. Blend remaining flour with port or wine, stir into casserole and cook until gravy has thickened. Meanwhile make stuffing, form into balls and fry until brown. Remove herbs from casserole and garnish with forcemeat balls. Serve with redcurrant jelly.

Braised Pigeons

2 young pigeons	pinch pepper
2 oz dripping	1 oz plain flour
2 medium onions	10 oz can consommé
1 large carrot	¼ pt water
1 leek	bouquet garni
¼ tsp salt	4–6 rashers streaky bacon

Preparation: 25 min   **Average cost: 45p**
Cooking: 2 hr   **Serves: 4**

Halve pigeons and fry in melted fat until well browned. Put into casserole. Peel and slice vegetables and brown in fat, stir in salt and pepper. Put into casserole, stand pigeons on vegetables. Add flour to pan and brown, stir in consommé and water, bring to boil. Pour into casserole, add herbs. Cook for 1½ hr at 350°F (mark 4) until pigeons are tender. Make bacon rolls with streaky bacon, bake for 10–15 min and serve with pigeons.

Pigeon Pie

4 pigeons	pinch salt and pepper
½ lb shin of beef	bouquet garni
4 oz bacon rashers	1 oz plain flour
1 medium onion	8 oz shortcrust pastry

Preparation: 30 min   **Average cost: 75p**
Cooking: 3 hr   **Serves: 6–8**

Halve pigeons, put into pan with shin of beef cut into 1 in. pieces, diced bacon, sliced onion, salt and pepper and bunch of herbs. Cover with 1 pt water, simmer for 1½–2 hr until tender. Remove pigeons and cut off breast fillets, discard remainder. Blend flour with 2 tbsp cold water, stir into pan and bring to boil. Put pigeon breasts and other ingredients into 2 pt pie dish (discard herbs). Make shortcrust pastry and roll into oval slightly larger than dish. Damp and put on pastry rim, damp and cover with remaining pastry. Flute and decorate edges. Bake for 20 min at 400°F (mark 6), cover with foil and cook for further 20 min at 350°F.

Casserole of Pigeons with Onions

½ lb belly of pork
2 pigeons
1 oz plain flour
12 shallots or small onions
12 button mushrooms

¼ tsp salt
pinch pepper
½ pt water
¼ pt red wine
bay leaf

Preparation: 30 min
Cooking: 1½ hr

Average cost: 85p
Serves: 4

Cut pork into 1 in. pieces and fry until brown. Put into casserole.
Cut pigeons in half, dip in flour and fry until brown, put into
casserole. Peel the onions, leave whole, fry in fat until brown, add
to casserole with mushrooms. Stir flour, salt and pepper into
remaining fat and brown. Gradually add water and then wine.
Pour into casserole, add bay leaf. Cook 1½ hr until pigeons are
tender. Remove bay leaf before serving with mashed potatoes.

Ragout of Rabbit

1 young rabbit
1 oz plain flour
¼ tsp salt
pinch pepper
2 oz dripping
2 medium onions
2 carrots

2 celery stalks
1 small turnip
¾ pt stock
4 tbsp parsley and thyme
   stuffing
4 bacon rashers

Preparation: 30 min
Cooking: 2 hr

Average cost: 70p
Serves: 4–6

Soak rabbit in cold water for 3 hr, dry and cut into pieces. Mix
flour with salt and pepper. Melt dripping. Dip rabbit into flour
and fry until well browned, remove from pan. Peel and chop
vegetables, fry until brown, put with rabbit. Stir remaining
flour into pan and cook until brown, gradually add stock and
bring to boil. Return rabbit and vegetables to pan and simmer for
1½ hr until tender. Make forcemeat balls with prepared stuffing.
Make bacon rolls. Fry bacon rolls, then fry forcemeat balls in
bacon fat until brown. Serve with ragout.

Rabbit Pie

1 young rabbit (2 lb)
¼ lb pickled belly of pork
1 onion
¾ pt stock
bouquet garni

1 oz plain flour
pinch pepper
2 tbsp chopped parsley
8 oz shortcrust pastry
milk to glaze

Preparation: 30 min
Cooking: 1½ hr

Average cost: 80p
Serves: 4–6

Soak rabbit and pork for 3 hr in cold water. Cut rabbit into pieces, remove skin from pork and cut into 1 in. pieces. Put into pan with chopped onion, stock and bouquet garni. Simmer for about 50 min until tender. Remove rabbit and pork to 2 pt pie dish. Blend flour with a little cold water, stir into pan, reboil, add pepper and parsley. Pour sauce over meat in pie dish, allow to cool. Make pastry (see page 36). Roll out a little larger than dish, make pastry rim, dampen edge, then cover with pastry lid. Flute and trim edges. Glaze with milk. Bake for 20 min at 400°F (mark 6), reduce heat to 350°F (mark 4), bake for further 20 min.

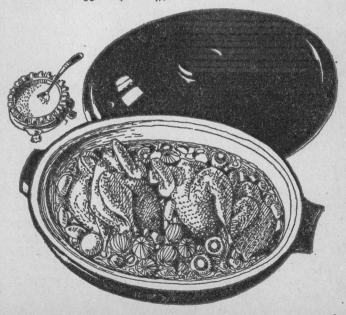

Turkey Tetrazinne

½ pt milk
bouquet garni
1 small carrot
1 onion
1 oz margarine
1 oz plain flour
pinch salt and pepper

8 oz cooked turkey
5 oz can button mushrooms
6 oz spaghetti
½ oz butter
2 oz fresh breadcrumbs
1 oz grated cheese

Preparation: 30 min
Cooking: 45 min

Average cost: 45p
Serves: 4

Put milk into pan with herbs and vegetables, bring to boil, remove from heat, cover and infuse for 30 min, strain. Melt fat in pan, stir in flour, gradually add flavoured milk, bring to boil stirring until thick, add salt and pepper. Cut turkey into 1 in. pieces, add to sauce with drained mushrooms. Cook spaghetti for 15 min in fast boiling salted water, strain, put into shallow fireproof dish. Spoon turkey mixture over top. Melt butter in pan, stir in crumbs and mix well, remove from heat, stir in cheese. Sprinkle over prepared dish, bake for 30 min at 350°F (mark 4) until brown.

Chicken and Ham Croquettes

¼ pt milk
herbs
1 small onion
1 small carrot
1 oz margarine
1 oz plain flour

pinch salt and pepper
6 oz cooked chicken
2 oz ham or cooked bacon
2 eggs
2–3 oz fresh breadcrumbs
frying oil

Preparation: 40 min
Cooking: 5 min

Average cost: 50p
Serves: 4

Heat milk with herbs and vegetables, infuse for 30 min, strain. Melt fat in pan, stir in flour and milk, cook until sauce boils, add salt and pepper. Chop chicken and ham, mix into sauce. Spread on plate, leave to cool. Cut into 8 pieces, roll into cork shaped pieces. Dip in whisked egg, toss in crumbs, pat into shape. Heat oil in frying pan, fry until well browned.

Chicken Pie

12 oz cooked chicken
1 carrot
2 onions
bouquet garni
¼ pt milk
1 oz margarine
1 oz plain flour

pinch salt and pepper
2 oz mushrooms
½ oz butter
4 oz cooked peas
8 oz shortcrust pastry
milk to glaze

Preparation: 30 min
Cooking: 30 min

Average cost: 65p
Serves: 4–6

Make stock with left-over chicken bones. Infuse carrot, one onion, herbs in milk for 30 min. Melt fat, add flour, cook for 2 min, gradually stir in strained milk and ¼ pt stock, bring to boil, add salt and pepper. Peel and chop onion, slice mushrooms and fry until tender in a little butter, stir into sauce. Cut meat into 1 in. pieces, mix into sauce with cooked peas. Put into 8 in. round oven dish. Make pastry (see page 36). Roll out, cut off pastry rim for dish edge, damp and cover with pastry lid. Flute and trim edges. Glaze with milk. Bake for 20 min at 400°F (mark 6). Serve hot or cold.

Ham Pâté

12 oz cooked cold bacon
    or ham
8 oz pork pieces
4 oz pigs liver
6–8 rashers streaky bacon
¼ tsp salt

large pinch pepper
¼ tsp marjoram
¼ tsp thyme
pinch nutmeg
1 clove garlic
2 tbsp sherry

Preparation: 30 min
Cooking: 1½ hr

Average cost: 85p
Serves: 6–8

Coarsely mince ham, pork and liver. Derind bacon rashers and line inside of 1 lb bread tin with them. Add spices and herbs to meats, with crushed garlic and sherry. Mix thoroughly and press into prepared tin. Cover with foil, put into baking dish filled with water and bake for 1½ hr at 325°F (mark 3). Leave to cool with weight on top. Serve cold with toast and salad.

Fish Chowder

12 oz fish fillet—whiting,
  haddock, plaice, cod
½ tsp salt
pinch mace
2 medium onions
2 sticks celery

1 oz margarine
1 lb potatoes
10 oz can corn
pinch pepper
2 tbsp chopped parsley

Preparation: 10 min
Cooking: 35 min

Average cost: 45p
Serves: 4–5

Remove skin from fish and cut into rough pieces. Put skin in pan with 1½ pt water, salt, mace and simmer 10 min, strain. Discard skins. Melt margarine in pan, fry chopped onions and celery for about 3 min, add peeled and diced potatoes, pour on stock, bring to boil and simmer 20 min. Stir in fish, corn, pepper and parsley, adjust seasoning and cook for a further 10 min until fish has cooked. Serve with crispy French bread and butter.

Baked Haddock au Gratin

1 lb haddock fillet or
  4 portions
8 oz pkt frozen spinach
¼ tsp salt
pinch pepper

2–3 tbsp milk
1 oz margarine
1 oz plain flour
milk
3 oz finely-grated cheese

Preparation: 15 min
Cooking: 20 min

Average cost: 50p
Serves: 4

Put 4 portions of fish into greased baking dish, sprinkle with salt, pepper and milk, cover with foil, bake for 10 min at 350°F (mark 4) until just cooked. Meanwhile cook spinach according to instructions on packet. Remove fish from dish, drain off liquid and put spinach into dish with fish on top, keep warm. Make liquid up to ½ pt with milk. Melt fat, cook flour, gradually add liquid, bring to boil stirring, add salt, pepper and half cheese. Pour over fish, sprinkle with rest of cheese. Brown under hot grill or in oven.

Poached Skate and Black Butter

4 portions skate	*4 tbsp vinegar*
2 pt water	*¾ tsp salt*
1 carrot	*2 oz butter*
1 onion	*1 tbsp chopped parsley*
bay leaf	*1 tbsp capers*
6 peppercorns	*pinch pepper*

Preparation: 10 min **Average cost: 50p**
Cooking: 30 min **Serves: 4**

Trim fish to good shape. Put trimmings into pan with water, vegetables, herbs, 2 tbsp vinegar, ½ tsp salt, bring to boil, simmer for 10 min. Put fish into a large flat saucepan, strain stock over top and simmer gently for about 15 min until cooked. Carefully remove to hot dish. Melt butter and heat until brown, stir in parsley, capers, salt, pepper and 2 tbsp vinegar. Pour over fish and serve at once.

Grilled Plaice with Tomato Sauce

4 medium whole plaice	Tomato sauce
1 egg	*1 oz margarine*
2 oz fresh breadcrumbs	*1 medium onion*
1–2 oz butter	*12 oz can tomatoes*
	1 tsp tomato purée
	salt
	pepper
	1 tsp sugar
	pinch herbs

Preparation: 10 min **Average cost: 50p**
Cooking: 10 min **Serves: 4**

Remove fish heads, wipe dry. Brush flesh of each fish with whisked egg and sprinkle with crumbs, press well in. Melt butter in grill pan, add fish—skin side down, dot with butter. Melt margarine in pan, fry onion until tender, stir in other ingredients, cover, simmer 10 min. Heat grill, cook fish until brown (about 5 min). Serve with sieved tomato sauce.

Surprise Fish Soufflé

2 oz carton potted shrimps
12 oz whiting
3 oz butter
2 oz plain flour
¼ pt milk

¼ tsp salt
pinch pepper
pinch mace
4 eggs

Preparation: 20 min
Cooking: 40 min

Average cost: 60p
Serves: 4

Grease 2 pt soufflé dish and put potted shrimps into dish. Remove skin and bones from fish, flake flesh. Simmer bones in ¼ pt water for fish stock, strain. Melt butter, add flour and gradually add stock and milk, bring to boil stirring while it thickens. Remove from heat, cool, beat in fish, salt, pepper, mace and egg yolks. Whisk egg whites to soft peak, fold into mixture, put into dish. Bake for 40 min at 400°F (mark 6). Serve immediately.

Stuffed Cod Cutlets

2 oz fresh breadcrumbs
1 tbsp chopped parsley
8 anchovy fillets
pinch pepper

2 oz margarine
1 small egg
4 cod cutlets
6–8 stuffed olives

Preparation: 15 min
Cooking: 12–15 min

Average cost: 60p
Serves: 4

Put breadcrumbs, parsley and half chopped up anchovies and pepper into bowl. Melt fat, pour spoonful onto crumbs and mix together with egg. Remove centre bone from each cutlet and replace with stuffing, tie each cutlet into shape with fine string, put into grill pan, brush with remaining fat. Cook through under medium hot grill. Just before serving criss-cross remaining fillets over top of each cutlet with few sliced olives. Serve with parsley or anchovy sauce.

Fish Timbale

12 oz whiting	*2 eggs*
1 hard-boiled egg	*1 oz margarine*
1 tbsp chopped parsley	*1 oz plain flour*
¼ tsp salt	*½ pt milk*
pinch pepper	*2 oz prawns or shrimps*
2 oz fresh breadcrumbs	*pinch salt*
4 tbsp milk	*pinch pepper*

Preparation: 20 min **Average cost: 60p**
Cooking: 45 min **Serves: 4**

Remove skin and bones from fish and cut flesh into ½ in. pieces. Mix with chopped egg and other ingredients. Bind together with whisked eggs. Put into greased 1¼ pt basin, cover with foil, steam gently for 45 min until firm to touch. Meanwhile combine margarine, flour and milk to make sauce, bring to boil, stir in prawns, salt and pepper. Turn timbale onto hot dish, coat with sauce. Serve with peas, beans or buttered carrots.

Plaice Sauté

4 rashers streaky bacon	*pinch pepper*
1 oz butter	*4 oz can pimentoes*
4 large plaice fillets	*1 (3 oz) pkt instant potato*
1 oz plain flour	*2 oz grated cheese*
pinch salt	*1 tbsp cream*

Preparation: 15 min **Average cost: 65p**
Cooking: 15 min **Serves: 4**

Derind bacon and dice. Lightly fry in pan until just brown. Remove and melt butter. Cut fish into 3–4 pieces, toss in seasoned flour and fry in fat until brown, turn now and again but do not break up fish. Drain pimento and slice thinly, stir into fish. Make potato as directed on packet and beat in cheese. Spread round inside edge of fireproof dish, brown under hot grill. Put fish in centre, spoon cream over top and put under grill for 1 min.

Fried Fish in Batter

Crisp fritter batter
4 oz plain flour
pinch salt
1 tsp dried yeast or
 ¼ oz fresh yeast
¼ pt warm water
1 tbsp oil

1½ lb cod or haddock fillet
 or skate, rock salmon
oil for frying
8 oz pkt frozen chips

Preparation: 20 min
Cooking: 10 min

Average cost: 75p
Serves: 4–6

Mix together batter ingredients, cover with damp cloth and leave 20 min in warm place. Cut fish into 8 portions, dry and sprinkle with salt. Put oil to heat in deep pan (oil should be 3 in. in depth). Have kitchen paper ready for draining. Prepare chips as directed on packet. Heat oil to 360°F (if no thermometer test by frying cube of bread 45 sec, it should be golden brown). Dip fish pieces into batter and slide 4 into hot oil, cook about 4 min until golden brown. Drain on paper and cook remainder. Serve with chips and tomato or tartare sauce.

Haddock Portuguese

2 medium onions
2 oz margarine
1 clove garlic
16 oz can tomatoes
¼ tsp salt
pinch pepper

1 tsp tomato purée
pinch sugar
1½ lb haddock fillet or
 4 portions
1 oz butter
1 tbsp chopped parsley

Preparation: 15 min
Cooking: 10 min

Average cost: 75p
Serves: 4

Peel and chop onions and fry in melted fat until tender, add crushed garlic, tomatoes, spices, purée and sugar. Simmer gently until thickened. Grease fireproof shallow dish. Put 4 portions haddock into dish. Dot with butter and cook 5–7 min under hot grill. When cooked through, spoon sauce over top and sprinkle with parsley. Serve with creamed potatoes or boiled rice.

Grilled Herrings with Parsley Fritters

4 medium parsnips	4 medium herrings
2 oz butter	oil for frying
1 tbsp chopped parsley	4 oz self-raising flour
pinch salt	pinch salt
pinch pepper	4–6 tbsp cold water
2 tsp lemon juice	

Preparation: 15 min   **Average cost:** 25p
Cooking: 10 min   **Serves:** 4

Cook peeled parsnips in boiling, salted water until tender. Drain, cut into ¾ in. rings, dry thoroughly. Beat together butter, parsley, salt, pepper and lemon juice, put to harden in a cool place. Clean and gut herrings, make 2–3 slits across each and cook under medium hot grill, turn when brown on one side. Heat oil about ½ in. in depth in frying pan. Whisk together flour, salt and enough water to form coating batter. Dip parsnip rings into batter, slide them into hot oil and cook until brown, turn over and brown on other side (fry only few at a time). Serve garnished with parsley butter and parsnips.

Fried Sprats Tartare

1½ lb sprats	4 gherkins
1½ oz plain flour	2 tsp capers
½ tsp salt	¼ pt mayonnaise
¼ tsp pepper	2 tsp chopped parsley
1 small onion	

Preparation: 15 min   **Average cost:** 30p
Cooking: 15 min   **Serves:** 4

Wash and gut sprats, discard badly damaged ones, dry thoroughly on kitchen paper. Mix together flour, salt and pepper, toss a few sprats in flour, shake off excess, and fry in a hot frying pan, sprinkled with a little salt (the fat from fish should be sufficient for frying). Cook for about 5 min. Keep hot whilst frying rest of fish. Meanwhile chop onion, gherkin and capers and mix into mayonnaise with parsley. Serve fish with sauce, brown bread and butter.

Soused Herrings

8 small boned herrings
¼ tsp salt
¼ tsp black pepper
pinch mace
2 bay leaves

2 small onions
6 peppercorns
¼ pt vinegar
½ pt water

Preparation: 10 min
Cooking: 40 min

Average cost: 30p
Serves: 4–6

Put fish skin side down on table, sprinkle with salt, pepper and mace. Put a piece of bay leaf and onion ring on each. Roll up herrings and fix with cocktail stick. Slice remaining onion and put into baking dish with peppercorns, vinegar and water. Put fish on top, cover with lid or foil and bake for 40 min at 350°F (mark 4). Allow to cool in liquid before serving cold with salad.

Fried Herrings in Oatmeal

8 small boned herrings
1–2 oz medium oatmeal
¼ tsp salt
pinch pepper
2–3 oz butter (unsalted) or
    vegetable fat

1 carton yoghurt
1–2 tsp made mustard
pinch salt
2 tsp lemon juice

Preparation: 10 min
Cooking: 10 min

Average cost: 30p
Serves: 4

Wipe herrings and dip into oatmeal, salt and pepper. Heat fat and gently fry herrings until brown on outside and cooked through (cook 4 at a time). Drain on kitchen paper, keep hot. Mix together yoghurt, mustard to taste, salt and lemon juice. Serve with hot fish. Alternatively serve hot mustard sauce or parsley butter.

Fried Mackerel with Mustard Sauce

4 medium mackerel
pinch ground mace
3–4 peppercorns
1 shallot
1 oz plain flour
pinch salt

2 oz unsalted butter
1 oz margarine
1 oz flour
1 tsp dry mustard
2 tbsp vinegar

Preparation: 10 min
Cooking: 10 min

Average cost: 45p
Serves: 4

Remove head and tails from fish and clean fish thoroughly, cut in half lengthways and remove bones. Put trimmings and bones into pan with ½ pt water, mace, peppercorns and shallot. Simmer for 10 min, strain. Meanwhile wipe fish fillets, dip in flour and salt and fry gently in melted butter until brown and cooked through. Put onto hot dish. Melt margarine, stir in flour, gradually add fish stock and bring to boil. Stir in other ingredients and serve with fried mackerel.

Crab and Egg Salad

8 standard eggs
2 oz butter
8 oz canned or frozen crab
    meat
2 tsp lemon juice
pinch salt

pinch pepper
¼ pt thick mayonnaise
lettuce heart
4 small tomatoes
8 stuffed olives
1 tsp capers

Preparation: 15 min
Cooking: 10 min

Average cost: 50p
Serves: 4

Hard-boil eggs, halve lengthways and remove yolks and sieve.
Soften butter, beat in yolks (leave some for garnish), crab meat,
juice, salt, pepper and 1 tbsp mayonnaise. Divide filling between
egg whites and press together in pairs. Arrange lettuce on a dish
and eggs on top. Decorate dish with sliced tomatoes and olives.
Just before serving put spoonful mayonnaise over each egg and
garnish with sieved egg yolk and capers. Serve with brown
bread and butter.

Mussels Vinaigrette

1 tbsp olive oil
2 shallots
1 large garlic clove
1 medium red pepper
6 medium firm tomatoes
pinch salt
pinch pepper
pinch sugar

2 tbsp wine vinegar
2 doz fresh cooked or
    bottled mussels
4 oz long grain rice
1 tbsp thick mayonnaise
1 oz sultanas
1 tbsp capers
½ cucumber

Preparation: 20 min
Cooking: 20 min

Average cost: 50p
Serves: 4

Heat oil and fry chopped shallots, crushed garlic and chopped
de-seeded pepper lightly. Stir in peeled and chopped tomatoes
and cook until mushy. Remove from heat, stir in salt, pepper,
sugar and vinegar, leave to cool. Mix with mussels and chill.
Meanwhile cook rice for 12 min in fast boiling salt water, drain,
cool. Stir mayonnaise, sultanas into rice, place on large dish.
Spoon mussels in centre, garnish with capers, grated cucumber.

Curried Crab

1 large crab
1 medium onion
1 medium cooking apple
2 tbsp cooking oil
2-3 tsp curry powder
1 oz plain flour
½ pt fish liquid

pinch salt
pinch pepper
1-2 tbsp mango chutney
6 oz long grain rice
parsley sprigs
lemon wedges

Preparation: 30 min
Cooking: 20 min

Average cost: 60p
Serves: 4

If crab is not dressed, remove 'dead mans fingers' (grey inedible sacs) and extract meat from shell and cracked claws. Wash shell and boil in ½ pt water to make fish stock, strain. Peel and chop onion and apple, fry until tender in hot oil. Fry curry powder and flour. Gradually add fish stock, bring to boil. Stir in crab meat, salt and pepper to taste and chutney, simmer for 5 min. Arrange cooked rice round inside edge of dish and pour curry mixture in centre. Garnish with lemon and parsley. Serve with extra chutney.

Crab Pancakes

4 oz plain flour
pinch salt
1 egg
½ pt milk and water
fat for frying
1½ oz margarine
1½ oz plain flour

¾ pt milk
1 large crab or 8 oz frozen or
   canned crab meat
1 tbsp horseradish cream
pinch salt and pepper
8 oz can sweet corn
1 oz butter

Preparation: 30 min
Cooking: 30 min

Average cost: 60p
Serves: 4

Mix batter and make into 8 small pancakes. Melt margarine in pan, stir in flour and gradually add milk. Stir until sauce thickens and boils. Remove from heat, stir in crab meat, horseradish, salt, pepper and corn. Divide filling between pancakes, fold into parcels and arrange in buttered fireproof dish. Brush with melted butter, cover with foil, bake for 30 min at 325°F (mark 3). Serve with hot green vegetable or green salad.

Mussel Stew

2 qrt mussels
1 large onion
2 cloves garlic
¼ pt dry white wine
¼ pt water
8 peppercorns

bunch herbs
2 sticks celery
2 large eggs
¼ pt single cream
2 tbsp chopped parsley

Preparation: 15 min
Cooking: 15 min

Average cost: 70p
Serves: 4

Wash and scrub mussels in cold water, discard open or damaged ones. Peel and chop onion, crush garlic, put into large pan with mussels. Add wine, water, peppercorns, herbs and celery. Cover with lid and bring to boil shaking frequently, and cook until mussels have opened. Remove from heat, strain off liquid and put mussels into hot dish. Boil liquid rapidly to reduce to just under ½ pt. Whisk together eggs and cream and stir in liquid. Return to pan to heat and thicken (do not boil), test for seasoning. When creamy, pour over mussels, sprinkle with parsley and serve at once with crusty French bread.

Salmon Fishcakes

8 oz can pink salmon
1 tbsp chopped parsley
¼ tsp pepper
8 oz mashed potato
1 oz butter

2 large eggs
1–2 tbsp brown crumbs
oil for frying
quick tomato sauce

Preparation: 15 min
Cooking: 10 min

Average cost: 30p
Serves: 4

Drain liquid from can and mash fish with parsley and pepper.
Make mashed potato and beat in butter and 1 egg yolk, mix with
fish. Divide into 8 pieces and shape into flat cakes. Brush with
remaining whisked egg and dip into crumbs, pat crumbs well
into fishcakes (repeat process again if wished). Heat oil and fry
fishcakes until brown on both sides. Drain on kitchen paper.
Make tomato sauce (see page 69) and serve at once.

Kedgeree

3 oz long grain rice
1 oz margarine
1 oz plain flour
½ pt milk
8 oz cooked fish
  (preferably smoked haddock)

pinch salt
pinch pepper
2 hard-boiled eggs
1 tbsp chopped parsley

Preparation: 20 min
Cooking: 15 min

Average cost: 30p
Serves: 4

Cook rice in fast-boiling salted water for about 12 min, strain and
rinse. Melt the fat, add flour and gradually stir in the milk until
sauce thickens and boils. Flake fish, discard bones and skin, stir
into sauce with salt and pepper. Stir in the rice, chopped eggs and
parsley. Reheat over gentle heat until well mixed and really hot.
Serve with crisp bread and butter.

Tuna Pie

2 medium onions
1 green or red pepper
1 oz margarine
¾ pt milk
1 oz cornflour

pinch salt
pinch pepper
12 oz tuna fish
8 oz shortcrust pastry

Preparation: 25 min
Cooking: 40 min

Average cost: 30p
Serves: 4

Peel and slice onions, slice de-seeded pepper. Melt margarine in pan, cook onions and pepper until tender. Stir in ½ pt milk, bring to boil. Blend cornflour to smooth paste with cold milk, stir into milk and boil. Add salt and pepper. Drain tuna and break into 1 in. chunks, stir into sauce. Make pastry (see page 36). Line 8 in. pie plate with half pastry, put filling on this, damp edges. Roll remaining pastry into round for lid, cover pie, flute and decorate edges. Glaze with milk, bake for 20 min at 400°F (mark 6) until brown. Serve hot with chicory and pepper salad.

Fish Pie

1 oz margarine
1 oz plain flour
½ pt milk or
    milk and fish stock
2 tbsp chopped parsley
2 hard-boiled eggs

1–2 tsp anchovy essence
8 oz cooked or canned fish
3 oz pkt instant potato or
    1 lb peeled potatoes cooked
    and mashed

Preparation: 20 min
Cooking: 40 min

Average cost: 35p
Serves: 4

Melt fat and cook flour. Gradually stir in liquid, bring to boil stirring. Add parsley, chopped eggs and essence. Flake fish, add to sauce and test for seasoning. Put into greased, fireproof dish. Cream potatoes and pile on top of fish mixture, spread with knife, and brush with milk. Bake for 40 min at 350°F (mark 4) until heated through and brown.

A mixture of fish—haddock, prawns, canned salmon, tuna, pilchards, scallops, anchovies, cod—may be used together to give a good flavour.

Fish Puff

2 oz margarine
¼ pt water
2½ oz plain flour
8 oz mixed cooked fish
1 medium onion
1 oz butter
1 oz flour

½ pt fish stock or milk
2 tomatoes
2 tsp chopped parsley
pinch salt
pinch pepper
2 eggs
2 oz diced Cheddar cheese

Preparation: 20 min
Cooking: 40 min

Average cost: 40p
Serves: 4

Melt margarine and add water, bring to boil and stir in flour, beat well until a ball of dough is formed, spread round pan and leave to cool. Flake fish, chop peeled onion and fry until tender in butter in another pan, stir in flour. Gradually add liquid stirring until sauce thickens and boils. Stir in peeled and quartered tomatoes, fish, parsley and seasoning. Beat eggs into dough in first pan until mixture is smooth and shiny. Stir in cheese. Spread round inside edge of greased 9 in. fireproof shallow dish. Put filling in centre. Bake for 40 min at 400°F (mark 6) until golden and well risen. Serve at once.

Egg and Bean Curry

2 tbsp desiccated coconut
1 large onion
1 medium cooking apple
2 tbsp vegetable oil
1 tbsp curry powder
1½ oz plain flour

2 tsp tomato purée
pinch salt
pinch pepper
1 tbsp sweet chutney
16 oz can baked beans
4 large eggs

Preparation: 10 min
Cooking: 30 min

Average cost: 25p
Serves: 4

Pour ¾ pt boiling water onto coconut and infuse for 10 min, strain. Peel and chop onion and apple. Fry in heated oil until tender. Stir in curry powder and flour, cook for about 5 min. Gradually stir in coconut water and bring to boil. Simmer for 20 min. Add purée, salt, pepper, chutney and beans. Mix well, pour into hot dish. Poach eggs in simmering water, until just set. Remove with draining spoon and put onto bean curry. Sprinkle with coconut. Serve with crusty buttered bread and salad.

Spanish Omelette

1 red or green pepper
1 medium onion
1 clove garlic
1 tbsp olive oil
1 large cooked potato

2 oz cooked ham
6 eggs
large pinch salt
pinch pepper
pinch mixed herbs

Preparation: 10 min
Cooking: 12 min

Average cost: 35p
Serves: 4

Chop de-seeded pepper and onion. Fry with crushed garlic in oil in large frying pan. When nearly cooked add ½ in. diced potato and cook until brown. Stir in ham cut into ½ in. strips. Whisk together eggs, salt and pepper. Pour into vegetables in pan and cook over very gentle heat. Stir constantly until mixture begins to thicken. Continue cooking until the eggs just set. Sprinkle with herbs. Serve at once cut into wedges with crispy French bread and butter and chicory salad.

Scotch Eggs with Tomato Risotto

4 hard-boiled eggs
1 oz plain flour
8 oz sausage meat
1 large egg
2 oz fresh breadcrumbs
1 medium onion
2 oz bacon rashers

1 clove garlic
4 oz long grain rice
16 oz can tomatoes
pinch salt
pinch pepper
2 tsp tomato purée
frying oil

Preparation: 30 min
Cooking: 30 min

Average cost: 35p
Serves: 4

Shell eggs, dip in flour and cover each one with a quarter of sausage meat. Dip in whisked egg and coat with crumbs. Peel and chop onion, dice bacon. Fry with crushed garlic in pan, when just brown, stir in rice and brown well. Strain tomatoes and make liquid up to ¾ pt with water. Stir into pan, add salt, pepper and purée. Simmer gently until rice has cooked and absorbed most of liquid, add chopped up tomatoes. Heat 2–3 tbsp oil in frying pan, gently cook Scotch eggs until well browned all over. Serve with eggs cut in half and placed on top of tomato risotto.

Eggs Florentine

2 8 oz pkts frozen leaf
  spinach
2 oz butter
1 oz plain flour
½ pt milk
pinch salt

pinch pepper
4 oz finely-grated cheese
1 tsp made mustard
2 tsp Worcestershire sauce
8 eggs

Preparation: 15 min
Cooking: 20 min

Average cost: 40p
Serves: 4

Cook spinach according to directions on packet, drain well and toss in 1 oz butter. Put into shallow fireproof dish. Melt rest of butter and make white sauce, add salt and pepper. Stir in half cheese, mustard and Worcestershire sauce. Poach or soft boil eggs and put onto spinach. Coat with cheese sauce, sprinkle with rest of cheese. Brown under very hot grill.

Egg and Bacon Puff Pie

1 shallot
1 piece carrot
bunch herbs
$\frac{1}{2}$ pt milk
6 oz cooked cold bacon or ham

6 hard-boiled eggs
2 tsp chopped parsley
2 tbsp cooked peas
7$\frac{1}{2}$ oz pkt frozen puff pastry
milk to glaze

Preparation: 20 min
Cooking: 30 min

Average cost: 45p
Serves: 4

Heat shallot, carrot and herbs in milk, bring to boil and infuse for 30 min. Strain. Melt margarine, add flour and stir in flavoured milk, bring to boil, stirring until it thickens. Cut bacon into $\frac{1}{2}$ in. pieces, mix into sauce with chopped eggs, parsley and peas. Put into 8 in. fireproof plate. Roll pastry into 9 in. square. Cut into 8 in. round. Use trimmings to make pastry rims for dish. Damp edges and put lid in place, press edges together, flute, glaze with milk. Make hole in centre and decorate. Bake for 20 min at 425°F (mark 7), cover pastry with foil after 10 min, when well-risen and golden brown.

Stuffed Ham Eggs au Gratin

1 oz margarine
1 oz plain flour
$\frac{1}{2}$ pt milk
pinch salt

pinch pepper
3 oz grated Cheddar cheese
6 eggs
8 slices shoulder ham (8 oz)

Preparation: 15 min
Cooking: 15 min

Average cost: 60p
Serves: 4

Make sauce with fat, flour and milk. Flavour with salt and pepper, stir in half cheese. Hard-boil eggs and roughly chop. Mix together eggs, parsley and 2 tbsp sauce. Put spoonful of egg mixture onto each ham slice, roll up and put into fireproof dish. Pour remaining sauce over top, sprinkle with rest of cheese. Brown under hot grill or bake for 15 min at 400°F (mark 6). Serve with hot buttered toast or hot potato salad.

Stuffed Eggs with Tomato Jelly

6 hard-boiled eggs
2 oz butter
2 oz picked shrimps or prawns
8 anchovy fillets
½ oz gelatine
4 tbsp white wine

¾ pt tomato juice
2 tsp Worcestershire sauce
pinch salt
pinch pepper
pinch sugar

Preparation: 30 min
Cooking: 12 min

Average cost: 60p
Serves: 4

Shell the eggs, cut in half lengthways, remove yolk. Soften butter and beat in the yolks, chopped shrimps, diced anchovy fillets and pepper. Stuff filling into egg whites and put in cool place to set. Put gelatine in small basin and soak in white wine, warm gently to dissolve completely. Stir into tomato juice, add Worcestershire sauce, salt, pepper and sugar. Put a little tomato jelly in dish, arrange stuffed eggs on this and when firm, pour in remaining jelly. Leave to set firmly. Serve chilled with watercress, lettuce, chicory or other green salad.

Cheese, Leek and Bacon Pie

6 oz streaky bacon
1 medium onion
2 large leeks
2 oz margarine
1 lb potatoes

pinch salt
pinch pepper
4 oz grated Cheddar or
   Lancashire cheese
¼ pt single cream

Preparation: 20 min
Cooking: 30 min

Average cost: 25p
Serves: 4

De-rind and dice bacon, peel and slice onion and wash and slice white part of leeks. Melt fat and fry until just brown and tender. Remove from pan. Peel and slice potatoes, cook gently for 10 min in boiling salted water until just beginning to soften. Drain well. Put half potatoes with other ingredients into a casserole, stir in salt, pepper, half cheese and cream. Mix well. Top with sliced potatoes and remaining cheese. Cover and bake for 20 min at 350°F (mark 4). Remove lid and cook for a further 10 min to brown cheese.

Cheese and Tomato Darioles

2 eggs
pinch salt
pinch pepper
¼ pt milk
2 oz fresh breadcrumbs

5 oz finely-grated cheese
1 large onion
1 oz butter
6 medium tomatoes
pinch sugar

Preparation: 20 min
Cooking: 35 min

Average cost: 30p
Serves: 4

Whisk together eggs, salt, pepper and milk. Pour onto crumbs, soak for 10 min. Stir in 3 oz cheese and spoon into 8 greased dariole tins. Steam very gently for 30 min until firm to touch. Fry peeled and sliced onion in butter until tender, stir in peeled and sliced tomatoes, salt, pepper and sugar and cook for about 5 min, until thickened. Put into fireproof dish, turn darioles onto tomato, sprinkle with rest of cheese, brown under hot grill.

Cheese and Artichoke Soufflé

1 lb Jerusalem artichokes
3 oz butter
2 tsp chopped parsley
2 oz plain flour
½ pt milk
pinch salt

pinch pepper
½ tsp made mustard
4 oz finely-grated Cheddar
   cheese
4 eggs

Preparation: 20 min
Cooking: 40 min

Average cost: 38p
Serves: 4

Peel artichokes and cook until soft (10 min) in boiling salted water. Drain well. Toss in ½ oz butter and parsley. Put into greased 2 pt soufflé dish. Melt rest of butter, cook flour and gradually add milk. Stir until sauce thickens and boils. Remove from heat, stir in seasonings and cheese. Separate eggs, beat yolks into sauce mixture. Whisk egg whites to soft peak and fold into mixture. Put into soufflé dish. Bake for 40 min at 400°F (mark 6) until brown and well risen. Serve at once with salad, green vegetable or toast and butter.

Pizza

4 oz Bel Paese or
   Port Salut cheese
4 medium tomatoes
8 anchovy fillets
8 stuffed olives
4 oz self-raising flour

1 oz margarine
4 tbsp vegetable oil
pinch salt
pinch pepper
1 tsp dried marjoram

Preparation: 10 min
Cooking: 15 min

Average cost: 45p
Serves: 4

Slice cheese thinly. Peel and slice tomatoes. Cut anchovy fillets into strips, slice olives. Mix flour and salt together in bowl, rub in fat, mix to a soft dough with water. Heat oil in 8–9 in. frying pan. Knead dough into 8 in. round. Drop into hot oil and fry until dough rises, base turns golden brown. Turn over and cover with tomatoes, cheese, sprinkle with salt, pepper, marjoram. Arrange anchovies, olives on top, cover, cook gently for 6–8 min.

Kidney Gougère

2 oz streaky bacon
4 lambs kidneys
1 oz plain flour
1 medium onion
2 oz button mushrooms
1 large tomato
¼ pt stock

pinch salt
pinch pepper
1½ oz margarine
¼ pt water
2½ oz plain flour
2 eggs
2 oz diced cheese

Preparation: 20 min
Cooking: 35 min

Average cost: 40p
Serves: 4

Dice de-rinded bacon and fry gently until brown. Remove from pan. Skin, halve and remove core from kidneys. Toss in flour and fry in bacon fat until just cooked (about 5 min). Remove. Gently fry sliced onion, mushrooms and peeled and quartered tomato, stir in flour and stock, bring to boil and season. Melt margarine, stir in water and boil. Add flour, cook and stir until a ball is formed, cool slightly, then beat in eggs until smooth and shiny. Stir in diced cheese. Grease 9 in. fireproof dish, spread gougère mixture round inside edge. Put kidney filling in centre. Bake for 35 min at 425°F (mark 7) until well-risen, brown and crisp.

Cheese and Haddock Flan

4 oz plain flour
pinch salt
2 oz margarine, lard or
  vegetable fat
2 oz grated cheese
1 tbsp cold water
1 large finnan haddock (8 oz)

2 oz sliced mushrooms
1 oz butter
2 eggs
5 oz carton single cream
4 oz cottage cheese
pinch pepper

Preparation: 20 min
Cooking: 50 min

Average cost: 60p
Serves: 4

Put flour and salt into bowl, rub in fat, stir in cheese, mix to a firm dough with water. Roll out and line 8 in. flan ring or sandwich tin. Cook haddock and flake. Fry mushrooms in butter and put with fish into flan ring. Mix together whisked eggs, cream, cottage cheese and pepper, pour into flan. Bake for 20 min at 400°F (mark 6), then 325°F (mark 3) for a further 20 min.

Macaroni and Bacon Cheese

4 oz bacon pieces
1 clove garlic
3 oz cut macaroni
1½ oz margarine
1½ oz plain flour
¼ pt milk

pinch salt
pinch pepper
pinch nutmeg
4 oz finely-grated cheese
4 peeled tomatoes

Preparation: 20 min
Cooking: 35 min

Average cost: 25p
Serves: 4

Trim bacon, cut into small pieces and fry lightly with crushed garlic, drain well and put into 1½ pt greased fireproof dish. Cook macaroni in fast boiling salted water for about 12 min until tender, drain well. Reserve ½ pt for stock. Melt margarine, stir in flour and gradually add liquid and milk, bring to boil stirring until sauce thickens. Add salt, pepper, nutmeg and half grated cheese, mix with macaroni and pour into prepared dish. Slice tomatoes and layer on top, sprinkle with rest of cheese and bake for 30 min at 375°F (mark 5) until heated through and brown.

Spaghetti with Fresh Tomato Sauce

8 oz spaghetti
2 tbsp olive oil
3 large cloves garlic
1 lb tomatoes
pinch salt
pinch pepper

pinch sugar
1 tsp chopped mint
1 tsp chopped parsley
2 oz butter
grated cheese

Preparation: 10 min
Cooking: 12 min

Average cost: 30p
Serves: 4

Bring a large pan of salted water to boil. Gradually lower spaghetti into water and simmer for about 10 min until just soft. Meanwhile heat oil in pan and fry crushed garlic for about ½ min. Peel tomatoes, cut into pieces and cook for about 3 min until just cooked and juice running out. Stir in salt, pepper, sugar and herbs. Drain spaghetti, stir in butter and serve at once with sauce and finely-grated cheese, preferably Parmesan.

Spaghetti Bolognese

1 medium onion	3 tbsp tomato purée
1 celery stalk	¼ pt white wine
1 carrot	¼ pt stock
2 oz streaky bacon	pinch salt
4 oz raw minced lean beef	pinch pepper
1 tbsp oil	8 oz spaghetti
2 oz chicken livers	finely-grated cheese

Preparation: 15 min   **Average cost: 40p**
Cooking: 45 min   **Serves: 4**

Prepare vegetables and chop finely. Chop bacon and fry in large pan until just brown and fat running out. Fry vegetables until brown. Stir in the beef and brown, adding a little oil if necessary. Chop livers and stir into pan and cook for 2–3 min. Mix together purée, wine, stock, salt and pepper, stir into pan, bring to boil and simmer for about 40 min. Cook spaghetti in fast boiling salted water for about 12 min, drain and add butter. Put spaghetti into saucepan, mix well and serve with cheese.

Cannelloni

6 oz minced lean pork	pinch pepper
2 oz minced ham	pinch ground nutmeg
1 tbsp oil	1 egg
1 medium onion	8 oz pkt cannelloni
1 oz fresh breadcrumbs	2 oz butter
5 oz pkt frozen spinach	stock
(cooked)	3 oz finely-grated cheese
pinch salt	

Preparation: 20 min   **Average cost: 50p**
Cooking: 30 min   **Serves: 4**

Mix pork and ham, fry in oil until browned. Fry chopped onion. Stir in breadcrumbs, spinach, mix with meats. Add salt, pepper, nutmeg, bind with egg. Boil cannelloni in salted water for about 10 min, drain well. Stuff pasta with meat filling, put into buttered dish. Put butter on top, pour in 4–6 tbsp stock, cover with cheese, bake for 30 min at 350°F (mark 4).

Lasagne

8 oz green lasagne
½ pt béchamel sauce
Bolognese sauce

4 oz finely-grated cheese
(including either Cheddar,
Parmesan, Bel Paese or
Lancashire)

Preparation: 30 min
Cooking: 40 min

Average cost: 60p
Serves: 4

Cook lasagne in fast-boiling salted water for about 12 min until soft. Put into bowl of cold water to keep the pieces separate. Make béchamel sauce (as for Chicken Pie, see page 67) and make Bolognese sauce (see page 90). Have ready finely-grated cheese preferably including Parmesan. Grease a shallow 1½ pt fireproof dish and arrange layers of pasta, béchamel, Bolognese sauce and cheese. Finish with good layer of cheese. Bake for 35–40 min at 350°F (mark 4) until heated through and brown on top.

Spaghetti Casserole

2 medium onions
1 tbsp oil
4 oz mushrooms
8 oz spaghetti
1 oz butter
12 oz can tuna

pinch salt
pinch pepper
pinch sugar
16 oz can tomatoes
6 oz grated Cheddar cheese

Preparation: 20 min
Cooking: 30 min

Average cost: 60p
Serves: 4

Slice onions and fry in oil until just brown and tender. Remove from pan. Fry sliced mushrooms and put with onions. Cook spaghetti for about 12 min, drain well and mix with butter. Break tuna into 1 in. pieces. Add salt, pepper and sugar to tomatoes. Arrange in layers in greased 2 pt casserole with cheese sprinkled between layers, finishing with thick layer of cheese. Bake for 30 min at 375°F (mark 5) until bubbling hot and brown on top. If preferred, bottled mussels, canned salmon or anchovies may be used instead of tuna.

Rice and Nut Salad

4 oz long grain rice
4 tbsp French dressing
  (see page 31)
4 eggs

12 oz can pineapple rings
2 oz walnuts
1 head chicory
2 oz picked prawns

Preparation: 15 min
Cooking: 12 min

Average cost: 40p
Serves: 4

Cook rice in fast-boiling salted water for 12 min, drain well and mix with dressing whilst still hot. Leave to cool. Hard-boil eggs, drain pineapple and dice two rings, roughly chop nuts and mix these with rice. Arrange chicory leaves and pineapple rings round edge of dish. Halve eggs and arrange on top. Stir prawns into rice and pile into centre of dish. Serve with crisp bread and butter.

Chicken Liver Risotto

2 medium onions
1 clove garlic
2 oz unsalted butter
1 tbsp olive oil
4 oz mushrooms
8 oz chicken livers
1 oz plain flour

6 oz long grain rice
1½ pt chicken stock
¼ tsp salt
pinch pepper
1 oz tomato purée
4 oz grated cheese

Preparation: 30 min
Cooking: 35 min

Average cost: 40p
Serves: 4

Peel and slice the onions, crush garlic. Fry in butter and oil until tender. Remove from pan then fry sliced mushrooms. Put with onions. Cut livers in half, dip in flour and fry gently for about 4 min, remove. Fry rice until brown then stir in 1 pt stock, seasonings and purée. Cover and cook for about 20 min, stir once or twice with fork. Return all ingredients to pan with rest of stock. Cook for a further 10 min, until stock absorbed. Pile onto hot dish and serve with grated cheese.

Stuffed Peppers

4 large red or green peppers
1 large onion
2 oz margarine
2 oz mushrooms
4 oz long grain rice
¾ pt chicken stock

pinch salt
pinch pepper
6 oz cooked chicken
12 oz can tomatoes
¼ tsp mixed herbs

Preparation: 30 min
Cooking: 1 hr 10 min

Average cost: 60p
Serves: 4

Cut tops off peppers, remove seeds and boil for 2 min in salted water. Remove, turn upside down and drain. Peel and chop onion and fry in fat, stir in chopped mushrooms and rice, cook for about 2 min. Add stock, salt and pepper, cover and simmer for about 20 min until stock has been absorbed. Dice chicken and stir into rice mixture. Stand peppers in fireproof dish and fill with stuffing, put lids in place. Mix together tomatoes, herbs and salt and pepper. Pour round peppers, cover with foil and bake for 45 min at 350°F (mark 4).

Rice and Salmon Mould

4 oz long grain rice
2 tbsp mayonnaise
8 oz can red or pink salmon
2 tbsp lemon juice
½ oz gelatine

¼ pt single cream
pinch salt
pinch pepper
1 cucumber
2 tsp vinegar

Preparation: 20 min
Cooking: 12 min

Average cost: 65p
Serves: 4

Cook rice about 12 min in fast boiling salted water, drain and cool, mix with mayonnaise. Drain salmon, make liquid to ¼ pt with water and lemon juice, flake fish and mix with rice. Dissolve gelatine in liquid and stir into rice with cream. Mix well, add salt and pepper to taste, put into 1½ pt ring mould or basin. Leave to set firmly. Slice cucumber, sprinkle with vinegar. Turn out mould and garnish salmon with cucumber. Serve with green salad.

Chicken Pilaf

2½–3 lb chicken
1 tbsp vegetable oil
2 medium onions
8 oz long grain rice
¼ pt single cream
¼ tsp salt

pinch pepper
¼ tsp mixed spice
1 tbsp lemon juice
½ pt chicken stock
1 red pepper

Preparation: 30 min
Cooking: 50 min

Average cost: 75p
Serves: 4

Cut chicken into joints and fry in oil until well browned. Put into casserole. Fry onion rings until brown and add to casserole. Cook rice in fast-boiling salted water for 12 min, drain well. Stir into casserole with cream, salt, pepper, spice and lemon juice. Rinse frying pan with stock and add to casserole. Cut de-seeded pepper into rings, overlap on top of dish, cover with lid and bake for 45 min at 350°F (mark 4). If dish gets very dry add extra stock or water.

Gooseberry Fool

1 lb gooseberries
2–3 tbsp water
3–4 oz castor sugar
2 eggs

1 oz castor sugar
½ pt milk
few cherries
double cream (optional)

Preparation: 15 min
Cooking: 15 min

Average cost: 15p
Serves: 4

Cook gooseberries in water until tender. Liquidise or sieve to a thick purée (about ¾ pt), stir in sugar to taste. Whisk together eggs and sugar, scald milk, pour onto eggs, return to pan and cook stirring all time until custard has thickened and is quite smooth. Leave to cool. When cold whisk together gooseberries and custard. Serve piled into individual glasses decorated with glacé cherries.

Whipped cream (¼ pt) may be used instead of custard or 2 tbsp may be stirred into fool before serving.

Other suitable fruits: blackcurrants, raspberries, apples, rhubarb, blackberries and bananas.

Rhubarb Fluff

1 lb young rhubarb
¼ pt water
2 oz sugar

1 large orange
2 oz seed tapioca
4 tbsp double cream

Preparation: 20 min
Cooking: 15 min

Average cost: 20p
Serves: 4

Cut rhubarb into 1 in. pieces and simmer with water, sugar and thinly-peeled orange rind until tender. Strain, remove orange rind. Put juice back into pan with orange juice and tapioca, cook gently until tapioca has cleared and juice thickened. Meanwhile purée or liquidise fruit. Whisk purée and thickened juice together then fold in whipped cream. Spoon into glasses and serve chilled.

Apricot Cream

16 oz can apricots
2 eggs
1 oz castor sugar
¼ pt milk

½ oz gelatine
grated rind 1 lemon
4 oz carton double cream

Preparation: 30 min
Setting: about 1 hr

Average cost: 27p
Serves: 4

Drain apricots and set juice aside. Reserve about 4 for decoration and sieve remainder with about 4 tbsp juice to make about ¼ pt thick apricot purée. Whisk eggs and sugar together and stir in milk. Return to gentle heat and stir until custard thickens. Remove from heat and cool. Dissolve gelatine in 4 tbsp juice and stir into fruit purée. Stir in cold custard, grated lemon rind and half the whipped cream. Turn into mould and leave to set firmly. Dip mould into hot water, turn onto dish and decorate with rest of cream and sliced apricots.

Blackcurrant Sorbet

8 oz fresh or frozen
   blackcurrants
2–3 tbsp water
4 oz sugar

½ pt water
2 tsp lemon juice
2 egg whites

Preparation: 20 min
Freezing: about 1½ hr

Average cost: 14p
Serves: 6

Cook blackcurrants with water until quite soft, liquidise or purée the fruit. Boil sugar and water together until sugar has dissolved. Cool. Mix syrup and juice purée together and make it up to 1½ pt with cold water. Turn refrigerator to coldest setting. Pour purée into freezing tray and leave until nearly firm (about 1 hr). Whisk egg whites until stiff. Remove frozen mixture from tray, put into bowl and whisk thoroughly. Mix in egg white, whisk thoroughly, return to tray and re-freeze until firm. Spoon into dishes as required and serve with crisp biscuits.

Raspberry Mould

12 oz fresh or frozen
  raspberries
½ oz gelatine

2 tbsp redcurrant jelly
4 oz carton double cream
2 bananas

Preparation: 20 min
Setting: 1–1½ hr

Average cost: 33p
Serves: 4

Sieve the fruit to make about ½ pt purée. Dissolve gelatine in water and stir in redcurrant jelly. When completely dissolved, stir into purée. Whip cream until thick, fold into fruit purée and pour into 1 pt mould. Leave to set, turn out and serve with sliced bananas.

Lemon Mousse

4 large eggs
2 oz castor sugar
¾ pt milk

2 lemons
½ oz gelatine

Preparation: 20 min
Setting: about 1 hr

Average cost: 20p
Serves: 4

Separate two eggs and put the whites aside to use later. Whisk yolks with other eggs and sugar. Scald milk with thinly-peeled lemon rinds. Strain onto eggs and sugar, mix well and return to gentle heat. Stir all time until custard thickens and is quite smooth. Turn into basin to cool. Put juice of lemons onto gelatine, leave for 2–3 min to swell, then stand in hot water until completely dissolved. Pour into cold custard and stir frequently until nearly setting. Whisk egg whites till standing in soft peaks and fold into setting custard. Pour into 1 pt ring mould or dish. Serve with sliced pineapple, fresh raspberries or sponge fingers.

Strawberry Whip

1 pt strawberry jelly
12 oz strawberries
2 egg whites
2 oz icing sugar

4 oz carton single cream
6–8 ratafia (macaroon)
  biscuits

Preparation: 40 min
Setting: about 1 hr

Average cost: 35p
Serves: 6

Make jelly as directed on packet, but using ½ pt water only, leave
to cool. Hull strawberries, keep half for decoration. Mash the
rest and stir into jelly. Whisk egg whites to soft peak, fold in
sugar and stir into nearly setting jelly. Fold in single cream, mix
until streaky. Pile into a dish. Decorate with remaining fruit
and ratafia biscuits. Leave until firm before serving.

Apple Snow

2 large cooking apples
1 oz sugar
1 tbsp lemon juice
2 egg whites

4 oz castor sugar
cherries
angelica
1 oz walnuts

Preparation: 10 min
Cooking: 10 min

Average cost: 14p
Serves: 4

Peel and core apples, slice and cook in pan with lid with sugar and
lemon until quite soft. Sieve or liquidise and cool. Whisk egg
whites to stiff peak stage. Whisk in half sugar and whisk again
thoroughly. Fold in rest of sugar and cold fruit purée; the
mixture should still remain thick and fluffy. Pile into a dish and
decorate with cherries, angelica and chopped walnuts. Chill
10 min and serve.

Strawberry Sponge

3 eggs
3 oz castor sugar
3 oz plain flour
12 oz strawberries

8 oz carton double cream
1 oz icing sugar
2 tbsp redcurrant jelly

Preparation: 20 min
Cooking: 15 min

Average cost: 36p
Serves: 6

Whisk eggs and sugar in a bowl over pan of boiling water until fluffy and thick. Remove and cool, whisking frequently. Fold in flour, mix well and put into 2 greased and floured 8 in. sandwich tins. Bake for 15 min at 375°F (mark 5). Turn out and cool on rack. Hull strawberries, keep half for decoration, mash remainder with fork. Whip cream until stiff and fold in crushed fruit and sugar. When sponges are cold split each in half and spread with jelly. Sandwich together with strawberry cream. Pile some on top, decorate with remaining strawberries. Serve chilled.

May be also made with raspberries and loganberries.

Stuffed Orange Salad

6 large oranges
3 bananas
8 oz green or black grapes

½ pt orange jelly
whipped cream

Preparation: 30 min
Setting: 1 hr

Average cost: 40p
Serves: 4

Cut tops off 4 oranges, scoop out flesh and chop into small pieces, discard pith. Cut bases of oranges so that they will stand firm. Remove skin and flesh from remaining oranges, put into bowl with sliced bananas, peeled and de-seeded grapes. Make ½ pt orange jelly as directed on packet, cool. When nearly setting, stir into mixed fruit. Fill 4 oranges, stand upright in dish and leave to set firmly. Serve chilled with whipped cream.

Marmalade Pudding

6 oz self-raising flour
½ tsp salt
2 oz fresh breadcrumbs
4 oz prepared suet
2 oz soft brown sugar

6 tbsp marmalade
2 eggs
4 tbsp milk
1 oz cornflour

Preparation: 15 min
Cooking: 2 hr

Average cost: 15p
Serves: 6

Grease 1½ pt basin and put a large pan of water to boil. Put dry ingredients into bowl, make hollow in centre and add 2 tbsp marmalade, eggs and milk. Mix well together and put into greased basin, cover with foil. Steam for 2 hr. Heat remaining marmalade and ½ pt water together until boiling. Blend cornflour with little cold water, stir into boiling liquid until thickened. Turn pudding onto hot dish and serve with marmalade sauce.

Cherry Cap Pudding

14 oz can cherry pie filling
4 oz margarine
4 oz castor sugar

2 eggs
4 oz self-raising flour
pinch salt

Preparation: 15 min
Cooking: 1½ hr

Average cost: 25p
Serves: 4–6

Grease 2 pt basin and boil large pan of water. Put cherry filling into prepared basin. Soften fat and cream with sugar until light and fluffy. Beat in whisked eggs and fold in flour and salt. Put carefully on top of filling. Cover with foil. Steam 1½ hr. Turn onto hot dish and serve immediately.

Jam Roly Poly

8 oz self-raising flour
½ tsp salt
4 oz prepared suet

¼ pt cold water
8–12 oz apricot, raspberry,
    gooseberry or plum jam

Preparation: 15 min
Cooking: 1½ hr

Average cost: 18p
Serves: 6

Put a large pan or steamer to boil. Put dry ingredients into bowl, mix to a soft dough with cold water. Knead dough lightly on floured board and roll into rectangle about 12 in. by 8 in. Spread jam to within 1 in. of edges. Damp edges with water. Roll up pastry, carefully enclosing jam. Wrap roly poly in foil, twist ends together to ensure wrapping is water-tight. Steam for 1½ hr. Carefully unwrap foil and serve on hot dish with extra jam if necessary.

Sultana Pudding

6 oz self-raising flour
½ tsp salt
2 oz fresh breadcrumbs
4 oz prepared suet
4 oz sultanas

2 oz soft brown sugar
2 tsp grated lemon rind
2 eggs
4 tbsp milk

Preparation: 10 min
Cooking: 2 hr

Average cost: 15p
Serves: 6

Grease 1½ pt basin and put a large pan of water to boil. Put dry ingredients into bowl. Mix to a soft dough with eggs and milk. The mixture should drop easily from spoon, add extra milk if necessary. Put into prepared basin, cover with foil. Steam for 2 hr. Turn onto hot dish and serve with custard.

Apple Pudding

8 oz self-raising flour
½ tsp salt
4 oz prepared suet
¼ pt cold water

2 lb cooking apples
2 oz brown sugar
2 tsp grated lemon rind

Preparation: 15 min
Cooking: 2 hr

Average cost: 15p
Serves: 6

Grease 1½ pt basin and put a large pan of water to boil. Put dry dients in bowl, mix to a soft dough with water. Knead lightly on floured board. Cut off quarter for lid, roll rest of pastry into a round large enough to line inside basin. Carefully lower into basin, press against edges, damp edges. Roll rest of pastry into a 5–6 in. round for lid. Peel and slice apples and put into prepared basin with sugar and rind. Put pastry lid on top, press edges well together. Cover with foil and steam for 2 hr. Turn onto hot dish and serve with custard.

Jam Layer Pudding

8 oz self-raising flour
½ tsp salt
4 oz prepared suet

¼ pt cold water
8–12 oz jam

Preparation: 15 min
Cooking: 2 hr

Average cost: 15p
Serves: 6

Grease 1½ pt basin and put large pan of water to boil. Put dry ingredients together in bowl, mix to a soft dough with water. Knead lightly on floured board. Divide into 6 pieces and roll into rounds, gradually getting larger to fit inside basin. Put a spoonful jam in basin cover with pastry round, build up in this way until all jam and pastry has been used. Cover with foil. Steam for 2 hr. Turn onto hot dish and serve at once.

Syrup Pudding

6 oz golden syrup
8 oz self-raising flour
$\frac{1}{2}$ tsp salt
1 tsp baking powder
1 oz soft brown sugar

3 oz prepared suet
1 tsp ground ginger
1 egg
4 tbsp milk

Preparation: 15 min
Cooking: 2 hr

Average cost: 15p
Serves: 6

Grease 1$\frac{1}{2}$ pt basin and put a large pan of water to boil. Put 2 tbsp syrup into basin. Put all dry ingredients into bowl, make hollow in centre and stir in syrup, egg and milk. Mix thoroughly and put into prepared basin. Cover with foil and steam 2 hr. Turn upside down onto hot dish, serve at once with extra syrup.

Chocolate Sponge Pudding

3 oz margarine
3 oz castor sugar
1 large egg
4 oz self-raising flour
$\frac{1}{4}$ tsp salt

$\frac{1}{2}$ oz cocoa
4 oz cooking chocolate
3 tbsp milk
1 oz butter

Preparation: 15 min
Cooking: 1$\frac{1}{2}$ hr

Average cost: 12p
Serves: 4

Grease 1 pt basin and put a pan of water to boil. Soften fat and cream with sugar until light and fluffy. Beat in whisked egg then fold in the sieved flour, salt and cocoa. Put into basin, cover with foil and steam 1$\frac{1}{2}$ hr. Just before serving, make chocolate sauce. Heat chocolate and milk together in small pan, remove from heat and stir in butter until sauce thickens. Turn pudding onto hot dish and spoon sauce over top or serve separately.

Apple Charlotte

6 oz fresh breadcrumbs
3 oz prepared suet
1½ lb cooking apples

2 oz soft brown sugar
grated rind of 1 lemon

Preparation: 15 min
Cooking: 1 hr

Average cost: 12p
Serves: 4

Grease a 2 pt pie dish thoroughly. Mix together breadcrumbs and suet. Press a thick layer round sides and bottom of dish. Peel and slice apples, mix with sugar and grated rind. Put apples into prepared dish. Cover with remaining breadcrumb mixture. Cover with foil. Bake for 45 min at 375°F (mark 5) until apples have cooked. Remove foil and cook for a further 10 min until well browned. Turn upside down onto hot dish, serve with custard.

Baked Jam Sponge

½ lb jam
4 oz castor sugar
4 oz self-raising flour
1 tsp baking powder
¼ tsp salt

3 oz soft cooking fat or
    margarine
2 eggs
2 tbsp cold water

Preparation: 10 min
Cooking: 45 min

Average cost: 16p
Serves: 4

Grease 2 pt pie dish and spread jam on base. Put dry ingredients into bowl and stir in eggs and water, beat well for about 1 min until well mixed. Put into prepared dish, smooth over top with knife. Bake for 45 min at 325°F (mark 3). Serve at once with extra jam or jam sauce.

Stuffed Apple Meringues

4 large cooking apples
1 oz walnuts
3 oz dates

2 egg whites
4 oz castor sugar

Preparation: 10 min
Cooking: 35 min

Average cost: 15p
Serves: 4

Wash apples and remove core from each. Make a slit round centre of each apple and, using a potato peeler, remove skin from top half of apples. Stand them in fireproof dish, pour a little water round dish. Mix together chopped nuts and dates, stuff into core cavities. Bake for 30 min at 350°F (mark 4) until just tender but still whole. Whisk egg whites to stiff peak, whisk in half sugar, fold in the rest. Spread meringue over each apple (or pipe if preferred) dust with extra castor sugar. Bake for 5–10 min until well browned.

Plum Crumble

1½ lb plums
2 oz sugar
8 oz plain flour

½ tsp salt
4 oz margarine or cooking fat
2 oz coarse brown sugar

Preparation: 15 min
Cooking: 1 hr

Average cost: 19p
Serves: 4

Wash plums, cut in half and remove stones. Put into greased 2 pt pie dish sprinkled with sugar. Put flour and salt into bowl, rub fat into flour until it resembles fine crumbs. Stir in sugar, mix well, sprinkle over fruit. Bake for 1 hr at 350°F (mark 4) until fruit has cooked and topping is golden brown. Serve with custard or cream.

Chocolate Fudge Pudding

2 oz nuts
4 oz plain flour
¼ tsp salt
2 tsp baking powder
2 oz castor sugar
1 oz cocoa

2 oz butter
8 tbsp milk
Topping
6 oz soft brown sugar
1 oz cocoa
½ pt water

Preparation: 10 min
Cooking: 45 min

Average cost: 15p
Serves: 4

Chop nuts and mix with dry ingredients. Melt butter and stir in milk. Add to dry ingredients and put into greased shallow dish approximately 7 in. by 10 in. Mix together brown sugar and cocoa for topping, sprinkle over mixture in dish. Pour water over top. Bake for 40–45 min at 350°F (mark 4) until firm to touch. Serve at once with whipped cream.

Baked Banana Fluff

4 trifle sponge cakes
2 tbsp apricot jam
2 eggs
1 oz castor sugar

½ pt milk
6 bananas
2 oz castor sugar

Preparation: 15 min
Cooking: 40 min

Average cost: 24p
Serves: 4–6

Split sponge cakes in half and spread with jam. Whisk together egg yolks and sugar, stir in milk and pour over the sponges, leave to stand for about 5 min. Halve 4 bananas lengthways and arrange over top. Cover with foil, bake for 30 min at 350°F (mark 4) until sponge custard has set. Whisk egg whites to stiff peak, mash banana and whisk into egg white with sugar. Pile onto prepared dish, bake for 5–10 min until brown. Serve hot or cold.

Blackberry and Apple Pie

1½ lb cooking apples
8 oz blackberries
3 oz sugar
8 oz plain flour

½ tsp salt
4 oz margarine, cooking fat or lard
2 tbsp cold water

Preparation: 20 min
Cooking: 40 min

Average cost: 15p
Serves: 4

Peel and slice apples, put into 2 pt pie dish with blackberries and sugar. Mix flour and salt together in bowl, rub in fat until mixture resembles fine crumbs. Stir in water and blend into a stiff dough with round bladed knife. Knead lightly on floured board. Roll pastry ½ in. larger than pie dish, trim ½ in. strip from round edge. Damp rim of pie dish, put on pastry strip and damp. Cover fruit with pastry lid, seal and flute, make hole at either end of pie for steam to escape. Bake for 20 min at 400°F (mark 6), cover with foil and bake for a further 20 min until brown and fruit cooked. Serve hot or cold.

Coffee Walnut Mould

1 tbsp instant coffee
¾ pt milk
2 oz castor sugar
½ oz gelatine

2 egg whites
5 oz carton single cream
1 oz shelled walnuts
wafer biscuits

Preparation: 20 min
Setting: 1 hr

Average cost: 18p
Serves: 4

Heat coffee, milk and sugar together until completely dissolved. Soak gelatine in 2 tbsp cold water for about 5 min, then heat gently until dissolved, stir into warm coffee milk. Leave in cool place until on the point of setting. Whisk egg whites to soft peak consistency. When coffee mixture is almost set fold in cream, chopped walnuts and egg whites. Pour into 1 pt metal mould and leave to set. When firm, turn onto dish and serve with wafer biscuits.

Lemon Cream

3 eggs
3 oz castor sugar
¾ pt milk
2 lemons

½ oz gelatine
4 oz carton double cream
macaroon biscuits

Preparation: 20 min
Cooking: 15 min

Average cost: 25p
Serves: 4

Whisk together eggs and sugar. Stir in warmed milk, return to very gentle heat and cook stirring all the time until custard has thickened. Pour into bowl and cool. Stir in grated lemon rind. Dissolve gelatine in lemon juice and stir into lemon custard, mix well. Whip cream until thick, fold into nearly setting custard mixture and pour into 1 pt mould or dish. Leave to set firmly. Turn onto dish and serve with macaroon biscuits.

Caramel Custard

4 oz granulated sugar
2 tbsp water
1 tbsp lemon juice

4 eggs
2 oz castor sugar
¾ pt milk

Preparation: 20 min
Cooking: 1 hr

Average cost: 15p
Serves: 4

Put granulated sugar into heavy pan and heat gently until sugar browns and caramelises. Remove from heat. Add water and lemon juice and warm gently until caramel and liquid have combined. Pour into 1 pt heatproof mould or tin. Run mixture around base and sides until caramel has set. Whisk together sugar and eggs and whisk in warmed milk. Strain into prepared tin. Steam gently for 45 min–1 hr until firm to touch. Leave to cool before turning out.

Bread and Butter Pudding

3 oz thin slices bread
  and butter
1 tbsp marmalade
1 oz raisins

2 eggs
1 oz castor sugar
¾ pt milk
pinch grated nutmeg

Preparation: 10 min
Cooking: 45 min

Average cost: 14p
Serves: 4

Grease 1 pt pie dish or heatproof dish. Spread the bread and butter with marmalade. Cut off crusts and cut slices into triangles. Arrange in layers in dish sprinkled with cleaned raisins. Whisk sugar and eggs together in warmed milk. Strain over bread and butter. Allow to soak for at least 30 min. Sprinkle with grated nutmeg and stand dish in pan of water. Bake for 45 min at 325°F (mark 3) until pudding has set. Serve hot.

Chocolate Semolina Whip

1 pt milk	*2 eggs*
½ oz cocoa	*1 oz butter*
1½ oz semolina	*1 oz dessert chocolate*
1 oz castor sugar	

Preparation: 20 min
Cooking: 10 min

Average cost: 15p
Serves: 4

Heat milk and cocoa in pan to nearly boiling point. Sprinkle in semolina and cook, stirring thoroughly until mixture thickens and boils. Cook for further 5 min stirring all the time. Remove from heat and stir in sugar, whisked egg yolks and butter. Leave to cool about 30 min. Whisk egg whites to soft peak and whisk into chocolate semolina. Pile into glass dish or individual glasses and sprinkle with grated chocolate before serving.

Imperial Rice

3 oz pudding rice	*½ oz gelatine*
1½ pt milk	*2 tbsp cold water*
1 tsp vanilla essence	*1 oz glacé cherries and angelica*
4 oz castor sugar	*4 oz carton double cream*
2 eggs	*16 oz can apricots*

Preparation: 40 min
Cooking: 45 min

Average cost: 30p
Serves: 4–6

Put rice and 1 pt milk into double saucepan (or basin over hot water) and cook until rice is soft and milk absorbed. Remove from heat, stir in vanilla and half sugar and leave to cool. Meanwhile whisk eggs and remaining sugar together, stir in rest of warmed milk. Return to pan and cook very gently, stirring all the time until custard has thickened (do not boil). Cool. Dissolve gelatine in water and stir into rice with chopped cherries, angelica and custard. Whip cream until thick. When rice mixture has nearly set, fold in cream and pour into 1½ pt mould. When set, turn onto dish and serve with canned apricots.

Strawberry Tapioca Cream

1 pt milk
2 oz seed tapioca
1 oz castor sugar
1 tsp grated lemon rind

2 eggs
12 oz strawberry jam
4 oz carton double cream

Preparation: 20 min
Cooking: 30 min

Average cost: 30p
Serves: 4–6

Heat milk to boiling point. Sprinkle in tapioca and stir well until mixture has thickened and tapioca is quite clear. Remove from heat, stir in sugar and grated lemon rind. Whisk egg yolks and stir into tapioca. Whisk egg whites to soft peak and fold into mixture. Put spoonful jam in base of glass dish, cover with layer of tapioca and repeat until all jam and tapioca cream used. Leave to chill. Whip cream, pile on top, decorate with few blobs of jam and serve with crisp biscuits.

Apricot Stuffed Pancakes

4 oz plain flour
pinch salt
1 egg
¼ pt milk and water

fat for frying
12 oz apricot conserve
or jam
1 oz blanched almonds

Preparation: 20 min
Cooking: 15 min

Average cost: 25p
Serves: 4

Put flour and salt into bowl together, make hollow in centre and whisk in the egg and milk. Beat thoroughly to a smooth batter. Heat a little lard or cooking fat (or butter) in small frying pan, when hot pour in thin layer of batter. Heat until set, then using palette knife turn onto other side and cook until golden brown. Turn onto hot plate and make 7 more pancakes. Put 2 tsp conserve into each pancake, fold into 4 and put into buttered, fireproof dish. Dissolve 1 tbsp apricot conserve in 2 tbsp water, pour over pancakes. Sprinkle with chopped almonds and bake for 10 min at 350°F (mark 4).

Orange Cream Fritters

3 eggs
1½ oz castor sugar
1¼ oz plain flour
½ pt milk
2 large oranges

4 oz cake crumbs
4 oz unsalted butter
½ oz cornflour
1 oz castor sugar

Preparation: 30 min
Cooking: 15 min

Average cost: 24p
Serves: 4

Whisk together 3 egg yolks, sugar and flour. Warm milk and stir into egg mixture. Return to pan and bring to the boil, stirring all the time. Remove from heat, add two whisked egg whites and grated rind. Mix well, then spread about 1½ in. thick on plate, leave to cool. When cold, cut into 8 pieces. Dip into whisked egg white and dip into cake crumbs, pat crumbs well into place. Fry until golden brown in hot butter. Drain on kitchen paper. Squeeze oranges and make juice to ½ pt with water. Blend cornflour with 2 tbsp juice, heat rest with sugar to boiling point, pour onto blended cornflour and re-boil. Serve fritters hot with orange sauce.

Chocolate Bavaroise

3 large eggs
2 oz castor sugar
¾ pt milk

4 oz cooking chocolate
½ oz gelatine
5 oz carton double cream

Preparation: 30 min
Setting: 30 min

Average cost: 40p
Serves: 6

Separate eggs. Whisk yolks and sugar together until creamy. Heat milk and chocolate together until dissolved. Pour onto whisked eggs, mix well and return to pan. Heat gently, stirring all the time until custard has thickened and is creamy. Pour into bowl and leave to cool. Dissolve gelatine in 4 tbsp water, stir into custard. Whip cream until thick and whisk egg white to soft peak. When custard is on point of setting, fold in cream and then egg whites. Mix well and put into glass dish. Leave to set. Decorate with grated chocolate.

Trifle

6–8 sponge cakes
2 tbsp jam
4 tbsp sherry
2 large eggs
2 oz castor sugar

¾ pt milk
4 oz carton double cream
6–8 blanched almonds
6–8 glacé cherries

Preparation: 30 min
Cooking: 15 min

Average cost: 50p
Serves: 4–6

Cut sponge cakes in half and spread with jam. Cut into fingers and put into glass dish. Sprinkle with sherry. Whisk eggs and sugar together, pour on heated milk, return to pan and heat gently stirring all the time until custard has thickened. Remove and cool. Put the custard onto the sponge cakes and leave to soak for 2–3 hr, to settle and get firm. Whip cream until stiff, brown almonds and slice cherries and use to decorate trifle. Serve chilled.

Queen of Puddings

½ pt milk
3 oz fresh breadcrumbs
3 oz castor sugar

1 lemon
2 large eggs
2 tbsp raspberry jam

Preparation: 20 min
Cooking: 1 hr

Average cost: 14p
Serves: 4

Heat the milk, pour onto breadcrumbs and leave to soak for about 10 min. Stir in 1 tbsp sugar, grated lemon rind and egg yolks. Put into greased 1 pt pie dish. Bake for 20 min at 325°F (mark 3) until just firm. Remove from oven, spread with jam. Whisk egg whites to a stiff peak and whisk in remaining sugar. Pile onto pudding, return to oven for 30 min until brown and crisp.

Mandarin Crumb Flan

4 oz sweetmeal biscuits
2 oz unsalted butter
12 oz can mandarin oranges

½ oz gelatine
5 oz carton yoghurt
1 oz soft brown sugar

Preparation: 10 min
Cooking: t/c

Average cost: 25p
Serves: 4

Crush the biscuits with rolling pin, put into a bowl and stir in melted butter. Mix well, then press into a 7 in. loose based flan ring, pressing well against the sides. Put in cool place to set firmly. Drain can of mandarins and dissolve gelatine in liquid. Stir gelatine into yoghurt and sugar, mix well and stir in half orange segments. Put into prepared flan ring and leave to set. Decorate with remaining segments and serve chilled.

Cabinet Pudding

3 oz stale sponge or
   Madeira cake
½ oz glacé cherries
½ oz raisins
2 eggs

1 oz castor sugar
1 tsp vanilla essence
½ pt milk
2 tbsp apricot jam
4 tbsp water

Preparation: 15 min
Cooking: 45 min

Average cost: 20p
Serves: 4

Cut cake into ¾ in. dice. Grease 1½ pt basin and decorate sides and base with cherries and raisins. Put cake into basin. Whisk eggs, sugar and essence together, whisk in the milk. Strain over diced cake and leave to soak for 1 hr. Cover with foil and steam very gently for 45 min or until firm to touch. Heat jam and water together and sieve. Turn pudding onto hot dish and pour apricot sauce round dish. Serve at once.

Chocolate Cups

4 oz cooking chocolate
4 oz stale sponge cake
2 oz chopped dates, raisins
 sultanas, cherries or nuts
2 tbsp sieved chestnuts or
 chestnut purée

3 tbsp apricot, plum or
 greengage jam
4 oz carton double cream
angelica

Preparation: 20 min
Cooking: t/c

Average cost: 30p
Serves: 6

Put chocolate in basin and melt over pan of hot water. Using a teaspoon, line 6 foil or paper cake cases with melted chocolate. Leave to set firmly in a cool place. Sieve the cake crumbs and mix with fruit and chestnut purée. Stir in jam. Fill into chocolate cases. Remove paper or foil outer skin and stand cups on a dish. Whip cream and spoon or pipe into chocolate cups. Decorate with angelica and serve chilled.

Viennoise Pudding

3 oz granulated sugar
1 pt milk
4 oz stale bread
2 oz soft brown sugar
3 eggs
2 tbsp sherry

2 oz sultanas
1 oz candied peel
grated lemon rind
½ oz cornflour
1 oz butter

Preparation: 30 min
Cooking: 1 hr

Average cost: 25p
Serves: 4

Heat sugar in thick pan until well-browned. Remove from heat and add the milk—reheat gently until all caramel has dissolved. Pour half onto the diced bread and leave to soak for 20 min. Whisk sugar and eggs together, stir in sherry and mix with soaked bread, sultanas, peel and lemon rind. Put into greased 1½ pt basin and steam gently for 1 hr until firm to touch. Meanwhile blend cornflour with a little remaining caramel milk, put rest to boil. Mix together and reboil with the butter. Turn pudding onto hot dish and serve with butterscotch sauce.

Quick Sponge Sandwich

4 oz self-raising flour
¼ tsp salt
1 tsp baking powder
4½ oz castor sugar
3 oz soft cooking fat or
    soft margarine

2 eggs
1 tbsp cold water
jam

Preparation: 5 min
Cooking: 25 min

Average cost: 12p
Serves: 6

Grease and flour two 7 in. sandwich tins. Put all ingredients (except jam and ½ oz castor sugar) into a bowl. Mix altogether with wooden spoon until smooth and thoroughly blended. Spread in the two prepared tins. Bake for 25 min at 325°F (mark 3). Turn onto rack to cool. Sandwich together with jam and sprinkle with castor sugar.

Walnut and Sultana Cakes

2 oz walnuts
2 oz sultanas
4 oz self-raising flour
¼ tsp salt
1 tsp baking powder

4 oz soft brown sugar
3 oz soft cooking fat or
    soft margarine
2 eggs
1 tbsp cold water

Preparation: 6 min
Cooking: 20 min

Average cost: 15p
Serves: 18 cakes

Put 18 paper cake cases on baking tin. Chop walnuts and put with cleaned sultanas. Put rest of ingredients into bowl and mix altogether using a wooden spoon, until smooth and well blended. Stir in mixed fruit. Using teaspoon put mixture into paper cases. Bake for 20 min at 325°F (mark 3) until brown and well risen. Cool on a rack.

Chocolate Sponge Sandwich

4 oz margarine
4 oz soft brown sugar
2 eggs
3½ oz self-raising flour
pinch salt
¼ oz cocoa

Filling
2 oz chocolate or vanilla
   butter icing or
2 oz cooking chocolate or
4 tbsp sweetened whipped cream

Preparation: 10 min
Cooking: 25 min

Average cost: 16p
Serves: 6

Grease two 7 in. sandwich tins. Soften margarine and stir in sugar. Cream together until light and fluffy. Whisk eggs together, sieve flour, salt and cocoa together. Beat eggs into creamed mixture with a little sieved flour, then fold in remaining flour, mix well. Divide mixture into prepared tins, smooth with knife. Bake for 20 min at 350°F (mark 4). Turn onto rack to cool. Sandwich together with flavoured butter icing, melted cooking chocolate or 4 tbsp whipped cream.

Madeleines

4 oz margarine
4 oz castor sugar
2 eggs
4 oz self-raising flour

pinch salt
½ lb raspberry or plum jam
2 oz desiccated coconut
6 glacé cherries

Preparation: 25 min
Cooking: 20 min

Average cost: 18p
Serves: 12 cakes

Grease 12 dariole tins. Soften margarine and stir in sugar. Cream together until light and fluffy. Whisk eggs and beat into mixture with 1 tbsp flour and salt, fold in rest and mix well. Divide cake mixture between prepared tins and knock down so that mixture falls to bottom of tins. Put onto baking tray. Bake for 20 min at 375°F (mark 5) until firm to touch. Turn onto rack to cool. Sieve jam and heat until runny. Spread coconut on paper. Halve cherries. Put cakes onto skewer one at a time, dip into jam and roll in coconut. Stand cakes in paper cases, put cherry on top of each.

Cherry Fairy Cakes

2 oz glacé cherries
4 oz margarine
4 oz castor sugar
2 eggs
4 oz self-raising flour

pinch salt
4 oz icing sugar
2 tsp lemon juice
2 tsp water

Preparation: 20 min
Cooking: 20 min

Average cost: 13p
Serves: 18 cakes

Grease 18 bun tins. Cut cherries into pieces, reserve 18 quarters for decoration. Soften margarine and stir in sugar. Whisk eggs and beat into mixture with 1 tbsp flour and salt. Fold in rest of flour and cut up cherries. Spoon into prepared tins and bake for 20 min at 375°F (mark 5) until firm and golden. Cool on a rack. Put sieved icing sugar into bowl and mix to a paste with juice and water. Warm slightly until just runny. Spoon a little onto each cake. Decorate with cherry quarter, leave to set.

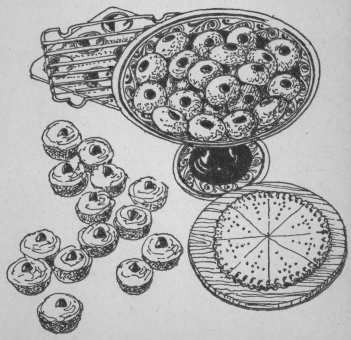

Shortbread

6 oz plain flour
pinch salt

4 oz butter
2 oz castor sugar

Preparation: 10 min
Cooking: 1 hr

Average cost: 10p
Serves: 8

Put flour and salt into bowl. Cut butter into small pieces and rub into flour until it resembles fine breadcrumbs. Stir in sugar, mix well then knead the mixture until it clings together in one piece. Put onto floured board and knead. Shape into a 7in. round and put onto baking tray. Crimp edges with fingers, prick with a fork and mark into sections. Bake for 1 hr at 325°F (mark 3). The shortbread must cook very slowly and should be just pale golden when cooked. Leave to set on tray for 2–3 min before cooling on a rack.

Melting Moments

4 oz margarine
4 oz castor sugar
1 egg
6 oz self-raising flour

pinch salt
½ tsp vanilla essence
2 oz rolled oats
24 chocolate buttons

Preparation: 15 min
Cooking: 20 min

Average cost: 12p
Serves: 24

Grease two baking trays and sprinkle with flour. Soften margarine, stir in sugar and cream together until light and fluffy. Whisk egg and beat into creamed mixture, fold in the flour and salt and stir in essence. Divide mixture into 24 pieces and roll into balls. Roll them in oats, put onto baking trays and flatten slightly. Press a chocolate button into centre of each. Bake for 20 min at 350°F (mark 4). Allow to settle on trays before removing on to racks to cool.

Oatcakes

7 oz fine oatmeal
pinch salt
pinch bicarbonate of soda

1 oz plain flour
1 oz bacon or beef dripping
boiling water

Preparation: 15 min
Cooking: 20 min

Average cost: 5p
Serves: 16–18 cakes

Flour some baking trays. Put dry ingredients together and mix well. Make hollow in centre and pour in melted dripping. Stir in enough boiling water to form a stiff dough. Knead well on floured board. Roll very thinly and cut into 16–18 triangles or 2½ in. rounds. Put onto prepared trays. Bake for 20 min at 375°F (mark 5) until oatcakes curl at edges and are crisp. Serve with cheese and butter.

Gingernuts

6 oz plain flour
pinch salt
2 tsp ground ginger
1 tsp mixed spice

½ tsp ground cinnamon
2 oz margarine
4 oz soft brown sugar
1 tbsp golden syrup

Preparation: 12 min
Cooking: 20 min

Average cost: 10p
Serves: 18 biscuits

Grease and flour baking trays. Sieve the flour, salt and spices together. Rub margarine into dry ingredients and add sugar. Mix well. Warm syrup and stir into mixture until a stiff dough can be formed. Roll into 18 balls about size of walnuts. Put onto prepared trays, flatten slightly. Bake for 20 min at 350°F (mark 4) until brown and crisp. Cool on rack.

Flapjacks

2 oz margarine
4 oz golden syrup

2 oz demerara sugar
8 oz rolled oats

Preparation: 10 min
Cooking: 30 min

Average cost: 7p
Serves: 20 biscuits

Grease shallow tin about 6 in. by 10 in. Melt fat in saucepan, stir in syrup and sugar. Stir in rolled oats and mix together. Press mixture into prepared tin. Bake for 30 min at 350°F (mark 4). Allow to cool slightly before cutting into fingers. Cool on a rack.

Chelsea Buns

1 lb plain flour
4 oz castor sugar
1 oz fresh yeast
8 fl oz warm milk and water
2 oz margarine

1 tsp salt
1 egg
2 oz butter
4 oz sultanas

Preparation: 30 min
Cooking: 15 min

Average cost: 18p
Serves: 18 buns

Mix quarter of flour, tsp sugar and yeast with milk and water, stir with wooden spoon and leave for 20 min until frothy. Rub margarine into remaining flour, stir in 2 oz of sugar and salt. Whisk egg and stir into yeast mixture, then stir in flour mixture and mix to a soft dough. Knead for about 10 min on floured board. Return to bowl, cover with damp cloth and leave to rise until about double in size (about 2 hr). Turn dough onto floured board and knead lightly (about 2 min) then roll into rectangle about 12 in. by 18 in. Brush with melted butter, sprinkle with rest of sugar and sultanas. Roll dough from longest side to enclose all fruit and sugar. Cut into 18 slices and stand them (open side up) on greased and floured baking tray. Leave to rise again for 15 min until puffy and springy. Bake 15 min at 400°F (mark 6).

Malt Loaf

2 oz cooking fat or margarine
4 oz golden syrup
4 oz malt
4 tbsp milk

8 oz self-raising flour
½ tsp salt
4 oz sultanas
1 egg

Preparation: 10 min
Cooking: 1¼ hr

Average cost: 12p
Serves: 6

Grease 2 lb loaf tin and line with greased paper. Melt fat in saucepan and stir in syrup, malt and milk, warm. Pour flour, salt and fruit into bowl and stir in warmed ingredients and whisked egg. Beat thoroughly. Pour into prepared tin and bake for 1¼ hr at 325°F (mark 3). After 20 min cover with foil to prevent loaf over-browning. Turn onto a rack to cool. Serve sliced and buttered. This loaf improves with keeping, leave unwrapped in airtight tin.

Doughnuts

1 lb plain flour	*1 egg*
2 oz castor sugar	*4 oz jam*
1 oz fresh yeast	*frying oil*
8 fl oz warm milk and water	*2 oz castor sugar*
2 oz margarine	*1 tsp ground cinnamon*
1 tsp salt	

Preparation: 40 min   **Average cost: 18p**
Cooking: 20 min   **Serves: 18 buns**

Make bun dough as for Chelsea buns as far as putting dough to rise for the first time. When dough has doubled its bulk (about 1 hr) turn onto floured board and knead for about 2 min. Roll dough about ½ in. thick and cut into 3½ in. rounds with cutter. Put 1 tsp jam in centre of each, gather up edges to enclose jam and roll into neat balls. Put onto floured tin and leave to rise (about 15 min) until puffy. Meanwhile heat oil in deep pan to 356°F (test by frying cube of bread to golden brown in 1 min). Carefully drop 6 doughnuts into oil and fry until golden all over (about 8 min). Remove and drain on kitchen paper. Roll in sugar and cinnamon and leave to cool. Re-heat oil and fry remainder.

Date and Nut Loaf

4 oz soft margarine	*pinch salt*
½ pt cold tea	*1 tsp bicarbonate of soda*
4 oz soft brown sugar	*¼ tsp ground nutmeg*
4 oz dates	*¼ tsp ground cinnamon*
9 oz self-raising flour	*2 oz walnuts*

Preparation: 15 min   **Average cost: 16p**
Cooking: 1¼ hr   **Serves: 6**

Grease a 2 lb loaf tin and line with greased paper. Melt margarine in saucepan, stir in tea, sugar, and chopped dates, bring to boil and simmer for 4 min. Cool. Sieve together flour, salt, bicarbonate of soda, nutmeg and cinnamon into a bowl. Stir in chopped walnuts, adding the melted ingredients and beat thoroughly until well mixed. Put into prepared tin and bake for 1¼ hr at 350°F (mark 4). Leave to settle in tin before turning onto rack to cool.

Swiss Buns

1 lb plain flour
2 oz castor sugar
1 oz fresh yeast
8 fl oz warm milk and water
2 oz margarine
1 tsp salt

1 egg
2 tsp grated lemon rind
8 oz icing sugar
2 tsp lemon juice
2 tsp water

Preparation: 30 min   **Average cost: 16p**
Cooking: 15 min   **Serves: 12**

Make the bun dough as for Chelsea buns but mix the lemon rind into mixture with whisked egg. Put dough to rise (about 1 hr). Knead dough on floured board for about 2 min. Divide into 12 pieces and roll each piece into sausage shape about 4 in. long. Put side by side on floured baking trays. Leave to rise until puffy and springy to touch. Bake for 15 min at 400°F (mark 6) until well risen and brown. Cool on rack. Mix icing sugar, lemon juice and water together and ice each bun. Leave to set.

Orange Teacake

2 oz butter
6 oz castor sugar
1 egg
2 tbsp milk
8 oz plain flour

½ tsp salt
2½ tsp baking powder
grated rind 1 orange
2 tbsp orange juice

Preparation: 15 min
Cooking: 45 min

Average cost: 12½p
Serves: 6

Grease a 1 lb loaf tin and line with greased paper. Soften butter and stir in sugar, beat together until well mixed. Stir in whisked egg and milk. Sieve together flour, salt and baking powder and stir into other ingredients with the grated rind and orange juice. Mix well and put into prepared tin, smooth top with knife. Bake for 45 min at 375°F (mark 5). Allow to settle in tin before turning onto rack to cool. Serve sliced and spread with butter or cream cheese.

Coconut Ring

2½ oz desiccated coconut
6 oz margarine or cooking fat
6 oz castor sugar
3 eggs
8 oz self-raising flour
½ tsp salt

3 tbsp milk

Glacé icing
4 oz icing sugar
1 tbsp cold water

Preparation: 15 min
Cooking: 1¼ hr

Average cost: 20p
Serves: 8–10

Grease 1½ pt ring mould. Sprinkle 1 oz coconut onto a piece of foil, put into oven to brown (about 3 min). Soften fat and stir in sugar. Cream together until light and fluffy. Beat in the whisked egg with 1–2 tbsp flour. Mix other dry ingredients together and stir into mixture with milk. Put into prepared tin, smooth top with knife. Bake for 1¼ hr at 325°F (mark 3), until well risen and brown. Turn onto rack to cool. Make glacé icing with sugar and water, warm slightly then dribble it over cake. Sprinkle with browned coconut.

Family Cherry Cake

6 oz glacé cherries
8 oz self-raising flour
½ tsp salt
2 tsp grated lemon rind

6 oz margarine
6 oz castor sugar
3 eggs
3 tbsp milk

Preparation: 20 min
Cooking: 1¼–1½ hr

Average cost: 32p
Serves: 8

Grease 7 in. round cake tin and line with greased paper. Wash and thoroughly dry cherries, chop roughly and mix with flour, salt and lemon rind. Soften margarine, stir in sugar and cream together until light and fluffy. Beat in whisked eggs and milk with 2–3 tbsp flour mixture, then fold in remaining flour. Mix well. Put into prepared tin, smooth top and bake for 1¼–1½ hr at 325°F (mark 3). Allow to settle in tin before turning onto rack to cool. Remove paper.

Farmhouse Fruit Cake

5 oz margarine or cooking fat
6 oz golden syrup
1½ lb mixed dried fruit
4 oz chopped mixed peel
¼ pt milk
8 oz plain flour
½ tsp salt

1 tsp mixed spice
½ tsp ground nutmeg
2 tsp grated orange rind
½ tsp bicarbonate of soda
2 tbsp milk
2 eggs

Preparation: 30 min
Cooking: 1½–2 hr

Average cost: 35p
Serves: 8–12 slices

Grease 7 in. round cake tin and line with greased paper. Melt fat in saucepan and stir in syrup, fruit and milk, cook gently for about 2 min, then remove from heat and cool. Put flour, salt spices and orange rind together into bowl. Dissolve bicarbonate of soda in 2 tbsp cold milk. Pour fruit ingredients into flour, add eggs and mix well. Lastly stir in dissolved bicarbonate and mix thoroughly. Put into prepared tin and bake for 1¾–2 hr at 300°F (mark 2). Allow to settle in tin before turning onto rack to cool.

Cut and Come Again

8 oz margarine
8 oz soft brown sugar
4 eggs
12 oz self-raising flour
½ tsp salt

8 oz dried fruit
2 oz glacé cherries
2 oz chopped mixed peel
1 tsp mixed spice
1 oz flaked almonds

Preparation: 20 min
Cooking: 1½ hr

Average cost: 45p
Serves: 20 slices

Grease a shallow baking tin about 7 in. by 10 in., line with greased paper. Soften margarine in bowl and stir in sugar. Cream together until light and fluffy. Whisk eggs and beat into mixture with 2–3 tbsp flour. Mix rest of flour with fruit, washed, dried and chopped cherries, peel and spice. Stir into cake mixture. Put into prepared tin and smooth top with knife. Bake for 1½ hr at 325°F (mark 3) until brown and well risen. Allow to settle in tin before turning onto rack to cool.

INDEX TO RECIPES